African Pyramids *of* Knowledge

Kemet, Afrocentricity and Africology

MOLEFI KETE ASANTE

Universal Write Publications LLC

African Pyramids of Knowledge: Kemet, Afrocentricity and Africology

Copyright © 2015 Molefi Kete Asante
All rights reserved.
African Pyramids of Knowledge/ Molefi Kete Asante
'The right of Molefi Kete Asante to be identified as the author of this Work has been asserted by him/her in accordance with sections 77 and 78 of the Copyright, Designs and Patents Act 1988.'

Book Designer: Author Support

For information:
For information email AdvisoryBoard@universalwrite.com
Website at www.UniversalWrite.com
Publisher: Universal Write Publications LLC

Mailing/Submissions
Universal Write Publications LLC
237 Flatbush Avenue, Suite 107
Brooklyn, NY 11217-5224

ISBN-10: 0982532709
ISBN-13: 978-0-9825327-0-6

ACKNOWLEDGEMENTS

I want to acknowledge three of my colleagues, Professors Maulana Karenga Ama Mazama, and Patricia Reid-Merritt, because they have inspired my work with their constant ability to review, evaluate, criticize, and revise the Afrocentric text. It is rare to have true friends and these have been sustaining anchors of friendship through many trials, difficulties and victories. We have not always seen eye-to-eye but we have never been outside of each other's gaze. I have many godchildren, Simphiwe Sesanti, Adisa Alkebulan, Michael Tillotson, Ariana Vora, Thanayi Karenga, Muswele, Tamu, and Kiamuya Musumunu, for whom I work to do my best as an African man; may they find strength and knowledge in this book. To my friends Jean Bertrand and Mildred Aristide, Vusi Gumede, Cheikh Tidiane Gadio, Garvey Musumunu, Tiamoyo Karenga, Reiland Rabaka, Omotunde Kete Asare nee Orlando Andres Pineda, Lusala Nkuka, Stanley Mkhize, Koumba Fakoly, Mubabinge Bilolo, Shadrack Gutto, Yoshitaka Miike, Jing Yin, Ana Monteiro Ferreira, Elisa Larkin Nascimento, Niyi Coker, Toyin Falola, and the late Abdias do Nascimento, I offer this book as a token of gratitude for intellectual encouragement in my endeavors. I must also acknowledge the many students that I have taught over the years; they have been the reason for much of my work and they continue to be the beacons that beckon additional scholarship. They are too numerous to name, but the ones who have followed the Afrocentric path know precisely whom I am talking about. An African proverb from the Nile Valley says, "I am a king by nature, a ruler to whom one does not have to give anything." It is in this spirit of richness because of friends and ancestors, the abundance of African and African American culture that I offer this volume, seeking nothing in return. The aim of this work is to confront oppressive discourse by offering a radical testament of African knowledge. Thus, this is an earnest attempt to provide a sense of clarity around the field that is now being called Africology. I give thanks to Amen for patience and I offer the spirits of Nubia and Yoruba, my distant forebears, the best of my thinking on these issues. My children, Eka, MK, and Mario, have my unconditional love. My grandchildren, Jamar, Ayaana, and Aion, came into the world with quickness for Africa and keenness for culture that promise a bright future. I respect and appreciate them for never bringing me disappointment and always giving me a reason to be better. In addition, I give thanks and praise to Ana Yenenga, my partner, who has been my main supporter in advancing my intellectual work and my companion in all things creative and victorious. Finally, this book would not be published without the constant vigilance and optimism of my publisher, Denise Ayo Sekai Rosier. I am eternally indebted to her for the confidence she has shown in my work and the vision she has for transforming society.

PREFACE

The Afrocentric method seeks to transform human reality by ushering in a human openness to cultural pluralism that cannot exist without the unlocking of our minds for acceptance of an expansion of consciousness. I seek to overthrow parochialism, provincialism, and narrow Wotanic visions of the world by demonstrating the usefulness of an Afrocentric approach, based on beginning with ancient Kemet, to questions of knowledge. Without a plausible ideology we can never march in the same direction; Afrocentricity is essential for the collective vision. I must alert you to the overpowering value of realizing an Africa truth that has been staring us in the face for thousands of years: the permanence of the pyramids.

There is nothing profound in such a pronouncement, there have been similar pronouncements by various other writers, but what is different, I hope, is the identification of the principal cause of the failure in those other formulations. In the West there have been theories and critiques that are fraught with problems whether you call them by the names of existentialism, phenomenology, structuralism, post-colonialism, or deconstruction. What we have come to know is that the proponents of these views have hedged their bets in a European worldview that is moribund when it comes to looking at the outside world. *They cannot truly grasp the significance of a revolutionary idea that would challenge the Euro-centric projection of its method as universal. However, the time has come for a total re-evaluation of both intellectual privilege and the assertion of European dominance in knowledge.*

There are several reasons for this state of affairs. The first is that the enthusiasts would be overturning themselves, a most difficult task, particularly if they believe that there is at least a little bit of good in their formulation. Secondly we are talking to and about a society or worldview that has dominated for 500 years. What would the philosophers of Europe mean by humanism except perhaps expanding to other Europeans, except perhaps to admit other peoples into the historical consciousness of Europe? But for Europeans to enter into a view, a perspective where they will be able to share with others in a world of plural perspectives is to ask them to submit to revolution. This is precisely why the French insist on everyone in the society adopting French habits and customs; they cannot bear to see difference because difference, for them, poses a threat to their place. But it is not so bad to have a plural vision in a nation. After all, the nation is not an ethnic affair; it is profoundly about acceptance of other people in a pact that however imperfect tends toward common civic objectives. In fact, it is a realism that must come in order to protect the Eurocentric view as one part of the human view. Anyone advancing an exclusively Eurocentric view as universal is apt to be disappointed because such a view is dead. There is a growing critique of hegemony and domination. No one will be a slave anymore. Nations have risen up against political hegemony in a challenge to the authority of the West. Oppressed people have turned the tables on their oppressors. The primitive hold that Europe once held over the world has crashed into the barricades of history and we are at a new turn in the world of ideas and knowledge.

The former enslaved are using every means possible to maintain their revolt against oppression; and in revolt, they overturn both their own victimization and oppression and the idea that Europe is supreme. But the project of human knowledge is even more; it is a search for method that will establish a base for further inquiry into the processes and the practices of human culture.

Afrocentricity, as an aspect of centrism, is groundedness that allows the student of human culture investigating African phenomena to view the world from the standpoint of the African. In addition, Afrocentricity, as Ama Mazama argues, is a paradigm and its implications are multifarious and constant.[1] Since the publication of Mazama's book, *The Afrocentric Paradigm,* the theoretical and critical works on Afrocentricity have exploded. The current book is in some ways bringing us into the 21st century with new avenues for research and critique.

I have divided the book into four sections: (1) The Intellectual Landscape, (2) A Mobilization of Ideas, (3) Confronting the Historical Situation, and (4) Asserting The New Cultural Reality. The idea is to examine what constitutes the discipline of Africology; secondly, to discuss the hallmarks of creative and philosophical origin as part of the critical process of African recovery; thirdly, to propose new ways to deal with the historical situation, and fourthly, to envision what innovative examination of agency can do for the interpretation of human phenomena.

CHAPTER ONE

The Intellectual Landscape

African resurgence will never take place until Africans champion a renaissance grounded in a new paradigm of dramatic narratives of victory.[1] I do not bemoan the contemporary intellectual landscape because there is no escaping the fact that few offers of illuminating dramas exist outside of the Afrocentric school of thought. But circumstances of nihilism, decadence, and fear are rooted in the inability of our intellectuals to tag our success to new methods of analysis.

The ancient people of Kemet (ancient Egypt) who lived along the banks of the Nile took advantage of whatever situation was presented to them by the river's flow. In our own time we must take full advantage of the definitional, critical, historical, and cultural conditions found in our societies. The African scholar must dip the gourd into the eternal stream of African history and analyze every conceivable activity for its utility and application for present and future generations. You must detach from Europe in order to see what your ancestors have done, as Kofi Asare Opoku, said. If the river was full of water, the Kemites used large barges to float stones to various sites. If the river had little water, they used heavy sledges pulled by hundreds of people over constantly replaced wooden rollers. Every day was one of decision-making in the best interest of society. We can do nothing less in recovering our historical stance toward the future.

I have maintained that the Eurocentric West is trapped, even in its best intentions, by its concentration on itself, its selfishness, its inability to draw a wider picture, and it unabashed drive for greed and materialism. Thus it becomes possible for Trent Schroyer writing in *The Critique of Domination* to begin his attack on a scientized Western civilization with a passage such as the following:

> "The critique of domination, or the reflective critique of socially unnecessary constraints of human freedom, is as old as the Western concept of reason. In classical Greek philosophy the notion of reason (*nous*) was developed in relation to the *seeing* of the invisible in the visible, or of the essential in the appearing."[2]

Schroyer's emphasis on the Greeks, who were intellectual children of the Africans, suggests why the Afrocentric method has another advantage over the critical theorists. Wilden, Habermas, Sartre, Marcuse and other important minds of the West, some not even Europeans, have tried to set out a critical theory with its ties to the Greeks, but alas, we have broken from that tradition. I have read the Eurocentric writers as a part of my intellectual history but since I share other classical traditions as well I have no reason to be trapped in the European past. Essentially Sartre and Marcuse found that the foundations of a critical theory associated with the concept of negative reason, that is, the knowledge of something because you know what is not, were elusive. Boaventura de Sousa Santos wants to point Europe toward an appreciation of what he calls the "epistemologies of the South" but as a way to re-assert Europe. My claim is one of freedom from the constraints of Eurocentrists in connection with critical theory; yet I do not claim that the final emancipatory moment will have come when Africans write an entirely new discourse. Stepping outside of the historical moment might permit new interpretations, new criticisms, ultimately the acquisition of new knowledge. This is why the recent works of Kimani Nehusi, Ana Monteiro Ferreira, Reiland Rabaka, Christel Temple, Michael Tillotson, Nilgun Anadolu-Okur, and Lusaka Nkala must be examined for their theoretical implications for those who would seek another path.[3] I have also been impressed, though with some critique, with the growing corpus of Lewis Gordon around Existentialism in which he argues that existence and meaning are important in the context of black liberation. There is nothing wrong with this formulation because Afrocentrists argue that black liberation must come from black agency; this is the Afrocentric intervention into the question of existence and liberation.

Nehusi is exploring the origins and connections of language and culture in the African world as a new way to assert our relationship with each other. This is valuable and useful documentation of the value of the ancient classical languages of Africa. In this work, he is joined by the Congolese writer, Lusaka Nkala. Ferreira, on the other hand, has contributed an outstanding work on theoretical approaches to the question of world knowledge and has advanced the idea that seeking the Afrocentric ethic might be the most appropriate avenue of transformation. Christel Temple and Anadolu-Okur explore the dimensions of literature and theater in regard to the development of a practical response to culture.

Taking the position that the reduction of agency is the practical result of those who seek to prevent Africans from exercising their legitimate goals, Tillotson has written a provocative treatise on the essential nature of the process. Perhaps no other writer has done as much as he has done to establish the mechanism for the prevention of black success. As we speak of white privilege in terms of white Americans; we can now speak of the impact of white privilege on Agency Reduction Formation as it applies to Africans. In almost all historical, social, or economic dimensions, one sees this situation at work.

INSIDE HISTORY

However, a person steps outside one's history with great difficulty. In fact, the act itself is highly improbable from the standpoint of true historical consciousness. There is no anti-place, since we are all consumers of space and time. There is, of course, the unknown that we presume. is "out there" until we know it by "being there." Our place is the constantly presenting and re-presenting context, the evolving presentation context, the perspective—that is, history to us.

Afrocentricity is a self-conscious obliteration of the subject/object dichotomy and the enthronement of an African vision. It is necessary to advance the intellectual movement toward a meaningful concept of place. In saying this I am challenging the Afrocentrist to maintain inquiry rooted in a strict interpretation of place in order to betray all naive racial theories and establish Afrocentricity as a legitimate response to the human conditions. All knowledge results from an occasion of encounter in place. But the place remains a rightly shaped perspective that allows the Afrocentrist to put African ideals and values at the center of inquiry. If this does not happen then Afrocentricity does not exist. What are African ideals and values? The answers to this question provide the arena for Afrocentric debate, discussion, and *endarkening*. The Afrocentrist will not question the idea of the centrality of African ideals and values but will argue over what comprises those ideals and values. The Afrocentrist seeks to uncover and use

codes, symbols, motifs, myths, and circles of discussion that rein-
force the centrality of the paradigm as a valid frame of reference
for acquiring and examining data. Such a method appears to go
beyond Western history in order to re-valorize the African place
in the interpretation of Africans, continental and Diasporan. It is
no secret that much of what parades as African have been interpreted only in the light of Europe, thus warping our understanding of theory and method.

A collection of data, for example, for an Afrocentric project
will consider cognitive and material systems, direct and indirect,
data-gathering measures, myths, video-recorded conversations,
and unobtrusive acquisition processes based on the African culture, e.g., the style of male address used in fervent greetings, unspoken cultural understandings about relationship to elders, and
so forth. Knowledge relates ultimately to some human interest
even if it is only to "see" the person who conceives a problem.

SETTING THE FUNDAMENTAL AFRICANIST QUESTION

The pyramids of Africa, not the *Odyssey* or *Iliad* of Homer, are the
initializing tokens of human intellectual inquiry into the nature
of being. Nothing captures the moment of human creative energy
with as much comprehensive intelligence as the building of the
pyramids. Consequently no human figure in the ancient world
looms as large or as important in the beginning of our knowledge
as Imhotep, the architect and philosopher of the Sakkara Pyra-

mid. Each pyramid was a massive text and a testimony of the brilliance of the Africans who build them along the Nile River. Marcus Garvey once said, "We must never stop learning."[4]

Consequently, the pyramids, in all of their complexions and adumbrations, must become the central fountain for the sciences and social activities of the ancient African world. Whether geometry or medicine, organization or construction techniques, architecture or astronomy, one sees in the building of the pyramids the master narratives of African civilization, and hence, the beginning of the built-societies of the world. Herein are the essential characteristics of the building blocks of modern knowledge.

Unfortunately the Africanists, much like Egyptologists, their counterparts who deal with ancient Egypt, tend to be Europeans whose interest in Africa serves European studies more than African studies. They were unable to see beyond Greece and their studies of Africa therefore are woefully inadequate and often uninteresting. Where Africans participate in such enterprises, for example, under the aegis of the African Studies Association, they are bound by the same protocols as the European scholars. Since 1990 the African Studies Association annual conferences have had fewer than ten panels dealing with (Egyptian) Kemetic traditions or the relationship of the Kemetic culture to the rest of Africa. One asks, "How can hundreds of scholars participating in intellectual conferences on Africa not discuss ancient Egypt, Classical Nubia, Beja, Meroe, or the impact of Nile Valley Studies on our contemporary understandings?" In fact, the African Studies Association's reaction to ancient Africa is in line with the emphasis that such scholarly conferences, such as the American Studies Association, place on examining the Greeks and Romans. One is inclined, however, to suggest that Americanists probably place more emphasis on those classical cultures than Africanists place on Kemet and Nubia. What many scholars who participate in African Studies do is *not properly African Studies* but European studies of Africa. This has little to do with the racial background of the scholar but rather with the perspective from which the person examines data.

Seeing Reality from a Different Place

On some commuter trains half of the seats face forward and half face in the opposite direction. Although you are moving in one direction, depending upon which way you are faced you get a different view of reality. In the face forward position you see things going. On some trains they have seats against the sides of the wall—in those cases you see things coming and going. Well, we are like that at this moment in history we see things from both vantage points—coming and going—and what we see going are the vestiges of a system of racial domination—it was a wrong headed system in the first place—what we see coming is a postmodern society that is sympathetic to diversity and committed to plural views. Thus, no longer can European studies of Africa parade as African studies; the overthrow of the dominating canon has already begun.

A person who studies the economics of Tanzania in an economic department and then completes a dissertation on some aspect of the Tanzanian economy cannot automatically be considered an Africanist. In fact, such a person is essentially an economist albeit an economist who employs the assumptions, predispositions and methods of economics to the Tanzanian economic sector. Application of the protocols of the economic discipline to an African nation is a matter of selection not of philosophical outlook, it is a matter of temperament not of methodological discipline, a matter of fancy not of perspective.

What is difficult for some people in the field to understand is that African American Studies is not merely a collection of courses on a particular subject matter different from other courses by concentration on African phenomena. However, by virtue of the work in the field it has become a variety of human studies in the prosecution of its work. Africology is a human science; it is committed to discovering all the ways Africans search for harmony in society. Unlike most Western social sciences it does not examine data from a distance in order to predict behavior. Unlike some other disciplines it is neither purely social science nor humanities but a merging of the two fields as well as the use of several approaches to phenomena stemming from the Afrocentric paradigm. While it is possible for the sociologist and the anthropologist to say that their fields contain nothing new, that is, nothing that is not treated in other extant sciences; the Africologist knows that the results of the Afrocentric perspective is so profoundly revolutionary in the field of knowledge that it virtually constitutes novelty.

LINES OF AFROCENTRIC INQUIRY

In the book *Kemet, Afrocentricity and Knowledge*, I had argued that cosmological, epistemological, axiological, and aesthetic issues frame the Afrocentric enterprise. I still accept this thesis and believe that it is valid. In this regard the Afrocentric method pursues a world voice distinctly African-centered in relationship to external phenomena. We are unable to gather meaning from our own cultural and historical background if we do not explore all the dimensions necessary for knowledge.

Although I recognize the transitional nature of all cultural manifestations of a social, economic or political dimension, I also know that in the United States and other parts of the African world, culturally speaking, there is movement toward new, more cosmo-cultural forms of understanding. The legendary educator Susan Goodwin has insisted that we need to explore dimensions of knowledge not necessarily discussed in the one or two levels of thinking found in the Western world. In fact, Northern Europeans may have abandoned the lessons of Kvasir much to their detriment. Actually the Norse god of knowledge was also associated with wisdom. This, of course, was long after the appearance of Djehuty also called Thoth. Nevertheless, meaning for the Afrocentrist in the contemporary context must be derived from the most centered aspects of the African's being. When this is not the case, psychological dislocation creates automatons, that is, robots; that are unable to fully capture the historical moment because they are living on someone else's terms. We are either existing on our own terms or the terms of others. Where will the African person find emotional and cultural satisfaction, if not in her own terms? By "term" I mean position, place or space. In the Kemetic sense or ciKam or mdwKam sense I mean *djed*.

COSMOLOGICAL ISSUE

The place of African culture in the myths, legends, literatures and *oratures* of African people constitutes, at the mythological level, the cosmological issue within the Afrocentric enterprise. What role does the African culture play in the African's interface with the cosmos? Are dramas of life and death in this tradition reflected in analysis? In the Diaspora the ubiquity of the dance finds its expression in life itself as a reflection on the periods of human history that have given a people its myths and ancestral narratives. Thus, an exploration of civilization, for example is central to any Afrocentric interpretation of cultural or social reality. Indeed the fact that the dance is a way of life in traditional society is pervasive because everything is a part of everything else. Agriculture is not separated from medicine and medicine is integral to every other sector of society. One cannot divorce agriculture from metallurgy or from ritual; everything is integrated and connected like the interrelationship of every aspect of the construction of the pyramids.

EPISTEMOLOGICAL ISSUE

The key to the epistemological issue is how do we ascertain what is important in our quest for truth and a workable version of human reality and how do we assess such knowledge from the standpoint of acquisition of intellectual value and virtue. We are aware that African people have dealt with every fundamental issue that we face in contemporary time in Africa's history. Political authority and moral respect are based on aspects of human relations: (1) those that demonstrate in their lives a commitment to African values, and (2) those that possess some personality exchange value, such as good character, decency, and resistance. These are some of the epistemological lines that lead to discovery. In addition, we seek to resist oppression, sexist repression, and economic subjugation, while at the same time promoting the exercising of economic activity by Africans and women. Liberation is never given over; it must be acquired, taken.

AXIOLOGICAL ISSUE

In the realm of African values we seek to uncover, as best we can, from books, articles, papers, and rituals the meaning of worthiness. Here the Afrocentrist must examine the logical judgments of sages, record the sage wisdom, and offer different approaches to the question of what is valuable and ascertain the dimensions of personality in the area of human exchanges. Since it is not a thing or an object that has value but people, we would want to discover what aspects of a person is appreciated. The question of value is at the core of the Afrocentric quest for truth because the ethical issues have always been connected to the advancement of African knowledge that is essentially functional.

Good. What constitutes good is a matter of the historical conditions and cultural developments of a particular society. A common expression among African Americans relates the good to the beautiful, "beauty is as beauty does" or "she's beautiful because she's good." The first statement places the emphasis on what a person does, that is, how a person "walks" among others in the society. The second statement identifies the beautiful by action. If a person's actions are not good, it does not matter how the person looks physically. Doing *good* is equivalent to being beautiful. The Twi language uses *oni onipa paa* to indicate the idea of goodness and humanity.

Right Conduct, therefore, represents a category of the axiological issue in Afrocentric analysis. The Afrocentric method isolates conduct rather than physical attributes of a person in literary or social analysis.

AESTHETIC ISSUE

Art is a representational form of human behavior. According to Kariamu Welsh (1985), the African aesthetic is comprised of seven aspects which she calls "senses." These senses are: (1) polyrhythm, (2) polycentrism, (3) dimensionality, (4) repetition, (5) curvilinearity, (6) epic memory, and (7) wholism.[5] These aesthetic "senses" are said to exist as the leading elements of the African's response to art, plastic or performing. Polyrhythm refers to the simultaneous occurrence of several major rhythms: Polycentrism suggests the presence of several colors in a painting or several movements on a dancer's body occurring in the context of a presentation of art. Dimensional is spatial relationships and shows depth and energy, the awareness of vital force. Repetition is the recurring theme in a presentation of art. The recurrence is not necessarily an exact one but the theme or concept is presented as central to the work of art. Curvilinear means that the lines are curved in the art, dance, music, or poetry—this is normally called indirection in the spoken or written art forms. Epic memory carries with it the idea that the art contains the historic memory that allows the artist and audience to participate in the same celebration or pathos. Wholism is the unity of the collective parts of the art work despite the unique aspects of the art.

AFRICOLOGY AND THE BASE OF THE DISCIPLINE

Centrism, the groundedness of observation and behavior in one's own historical experiences, shapes theories. Without this phenomenology there can be no effective Afrocentric theories. In this way Africology secures its place alongside other centric pluralisms without hierarchy and without seeking hegemony. As an academic discipline, Africology is sustained by a commitment to studying the life narratives, cultures, values, and possibilities of the African people trans-nationally and trans-continentally. Furthermore, it opens the door for interpretations of a reality base in evidence and data secured by reference to the African world voice.

The anteriority of the classical African civilizations must be entertained in any Africological inquiry. Classical references are necessary as baseline frames for discussing the development of African cultural phenomena. Without such referent points most research would appear disconnected, without historical continuity, discrete and isolated, incidental and non-organic. Indeed, one cannot have any proper understanding of the African world without reference, if only by assumption, to the classical history of Africa. In the West one would never assume to study literature without reference to the Greeks, whether one was Spanish, German, or English. Why would a person consider studying African literary or oratorical forms without reference to the classical civilizations?

THE GENERAL FIELDS OF AFRICOLOGY

There are seven general subject fields in Africology: *social, communication, historical, cultural, political, economic,* and *psychological.* A student of Africology chooses a research issue that falls within one or more of these subject fields. In any endeavor to uncover, analyze, criticize, or anticipate an issue, the Africologist works to utilize appropriate methods for the subject. To examine cultural nationalism, for example, within the historical or political subject field would require a consonant method for research. The same is true for an examination of the applicability of Pan Africanism in a region of Africa.

There are three paradigmatic approaches to research in Africology: *functional, categorical,* and *etymological.* The functional paradigm represents needs, policy, and action. In the categorical paradigm are schemes, gender, class, themes, and files. The etymological paradigm deals with language, terms of words and concept origin. Studies of either sort might be conducted in the particularly in social context of African people, libraries and archives, or laboratories. The aim is to provide research that is ultimately verifiable in human experience, the final empirical authority.

A student of Africology might choose to perform a study in the general field of history utilizing the functional paradigm. Or one might choose the general field of psychology and the etymological paradigm. Or one might study a topic in the general field of culture and use the categorical paradigm. Of course, other combinations are possible and the student is limited only by her or his ability to properly conceptualize the topic for study in an Afrocentric manner. Since Africology is not history, political science, sociology, the student must be well-grounded in the assumptions of the Afrocentric approach to human knowledge.

Scholars in our field have often been handicapped in their quest for clear and authoritative statements by a lack of methodological direction for collecting and analyzing data, choosing and interpreting research themes, approaching and appreciating cultural artifacts, and isolating and evaluating facts. As an increasingly self-conscious field African American studies has begun to produce a variety of philosophical approaches to the Afrocentric inquiry. These studies have served to underscore the need for solid methodological studies at the level of basic premises of the field and have become, in effect, pioneer works in a new perspective on phenomena. The Afrocentric psychologists led in the reconceptualization of the field of African personality theories. Among the early leaders of this field have been Wade Nobles, Asa Hilliard, Na'im Akbar, Frances Cress Welsing, Kobi Kambon, and others. Initially calling themselves "Africentric" scholars, these intellectuals trained in psychology, political science, history, sociology, or communication have explored every area of human behavior that impinges on the African experience. Their work has greatly enhanced the research questions in Black Studies. Other fields have not been as successful as the African psychologists.

The field of sociology has remained mired, since the time Durkheim lived on Rue St. Jacques in Paris, in a "social problem" paradigm that does not permit a fair interpretation of African data. From the days of E. Franklin Frazier the greatest of the sociologists, the field has experienced a sort of "double vision". What does a sociologist do when there are no deviant classes or societies? In the case of most African scholars in these fields, little knowledge of African Americans or Africans is available. They neither appreciate nor understand the significance of the Nile Valley or the historical response to European aggression for five hundred years. Locked in a Marxist paradigm they are unable to truly examine the nature of Eurocentrism from an African perspective since they often believe that African identity and concern with African questions of centeredness are quite "essentialist".

I have consistently argued that the Africologist must begin analysis from the primacy of the classical African civilizations, namely Kemet (Egypt), Nubia, Axum, and Meroe. No accurate understanding of African phenomena can occur without a reference to African culture. This means that one cannot write fully without a self-conscious attempt to place the historical enterprise in an organic relationship to African history.

Africology is defined, therefore, as the Afrocentric study of phenomena, events, idea`s, and personalities related to Africa. The scholar who generates research questions based on the centrality of Africa is engaged in a very different research inquiry than the one who imposes Western criteria on the phenomena.

The uses of African origins of civilization and the Kemetic high culture as a classical starting point are the practical manifestations of the ways the scholar secures centrism when studying Africa. Africology uses the classical starting place as the beginning of knowledge. This is why Afrocentric is perhaps the most important word in the above definition of Africology. Otherwise one could easily think that any study of African phenomena or people constitutes Africology. Just because a person says she is studying black people in Mobile, Alabama does not mean she is doing Africology; she could be doing Eurocentric studies or Negro studies. The enterprise, to be Afrocentric, must view the agency of African people.

THE REACHES OF THE AFRICAN WORLD

The geographical scope of the African world, and hence, the Africological enterprise includes Africa, the Americas, the Caribbean, various regions of Asia and the Pacific. Wherever people declare themselves as Africans with a commitment to the grand narrative of the African world, whether recently out of Africa or not, they are accepted as part of the African world. Thus, the indigenous people of Australia and New Guinea are considered African, though at an earlier age than Middle Passage Africans, and therefore, in a larger context, subjects for Africologists who maintain a full analytical and theoretical discussion of African phenomena.

Although the major regions of the African culture are Africa, the Caribbean and the Americas, even within those regions there are varying degrees of cultural and technological affinity to an African world voice. Africology is concerned with Africans in any particular region as well as all regions. Thus, Abdias do Nascimen-

to reminded us that Brazil specifically, and South America generally, provided an enormous amount of cultural, historical, and
social data about Africans. In Brazil, Zumbi, the greatest of the
kings of the Republic of Palmares, Luisa Mahin and Luiz Gama
are principal figures in the making of African American history;
in the Dominican Republic, Diego de Campo and Lemba provide cause for celebration; in Venezuela, Oyocta, King Miguel,
and King Bayano stand astride the political and social history of
the region; in Columbia, there is Benkos Bioho; and in Mexico,
no fighter for freedom was ever any more courageous than Yanga.

Africology rejects the Africanist idea of the separation of African people as being short-sighted, analytically vapid, and phil-
osophically unsound. One cannot study Africans in the United
States or Brazil or Jamaica without some appreciation for the
historical and cultural significance of Africa as source and origin.
A reactionary posture that claims Africology as "African Slave
Studies"" is rejected outright because it-disconnects the African
in America from thousands of years of history and tradition. One
way to advance African studies is to use all methods possible to develop useful ways to gather data about African people, including
musical, oral, written and documentary information. The work of
scholars will be greatly enhanced by oral and video records that
have become essential tools of analysis for contemporary African
American studies. On the other hand, studies in ancient African
present different challenges.

RECORDS AND PERSPECTIVE

Much of the data used in a reconstructive Egyptian primacy must be artifacts since written records are barely 6,000 years old. Although *homo sapiens* seemed to have appeared more than 250,000 years ago, the fact that permanent records are fairly new is a limiting factor in assessing with complete certainty what their existence was like during the early period. The records are abundant enough in certain concrete areas, however, for the scholar to examine the origins of African civilizations as never before. Of course, Afrocentric approaches to these records, written or material, must be advanced. For example, because written documents are not found in a certain area does not mean that written documents did not exist. In fact, the materials upon which writing was done may not have survived. Neither can we say that in societies of priestly writing where a limited number of scribes had the knowledge of text that writing was unknown. It may have been generally not practiced while remaining specifically the function of a small cadre of scribes. Nor is it possible to make any assessment of the origin of writing with any certainty. Speculative answers are heuristic but not definitive. Thus in any discussion of the nature of records in Africa or among African people we must redefine the approach, perhaps to see writing as a stage in human history much like the introduction of radio or television.

All authors tend to write about what is accessible whether they are novelists or scholars. Therefore Christian Thomsen's 1836 interpretation of societies moving from stone to bronze to iron age was applicable to Denmark, the model for its development, and not to Japan or Ethiopia. Definitions become contextual and experiential in terms of what the scholar knows; the more appreciation one has of other societies the less provincial the definitions should be. Of course, this does not always hold true, as it should. We now know, of course, that these contextualized definitions are often the results of ignorance and no area has been the recipient of this ignorance more than Africa. At one time the Europeans held that the earth evolved through a series of catastrophes and that human beings emerged after the last general catastrophe. Without an appreciation for depth in time of the human race, all material remains were generally seen as reflecting people the Europeans knew like Vikings and Phoenicians. Scholars are still trying to sort out the contributions of these seafaring people. Since the seafaring modern Europeans of the eighteenth and nineteenth centuries spent considerable time writing about the Vikings and Phoenicians they attributed to these people a wider array of material culture than was justified. Since we now know, however, of material artifacts that extend far beyond the 6,000-year history of the earth the European biblicalists once accepted as fact we are in a better position to assess the antiquity of African civilizations.

Paul Tournal is credited with using the term *prehistorique* in 1833 as an adjective but it was not until 1851 when Daniel Wilson wrote *The Archaeology and Prehistoric Annals of Scotland* that the idea of a discipline emerged. In fact, the idea behind prehistory seems to be when written records cease to be available as you go back in time you have prehistory. Because Europeans saw race as a primary concept in discussing civilizations and cultures we are frequently called upon to sort out the negations of Africa they identified with race theory. In fact, this should be the purview of white scholars who introduced these spurious concepts. Of course, we cannot now leave it to them to make sense out of the confusion they introduced. If this seems harsh, it is intended to point to fundamental problem of Europe's intellectual starting place. You have to start with the pyramids as foundational to all human knowledge.

Any Afrocentric methodology must explain racial characteristics in a realistic manner. To begin with we must admit the strategic ambiguity of this term as it is often used. For us race is not a biologically stable term but what is possible to discuss is the continuation of gene pools for long periods of time. In regard to Africa this means that the entire geographical continent from Egypt to South Africa and from Senegal to Madagascar has participated in the same gene pool for thousands of years. The oceans, West African and East African, constitute the biggest barriers to gene flow possibilities with the Mediterranean and Red Seas being relatively minor barriers. Although it is possible to have gene pool overflow in any direction it is most likely that the major oceans serve as fairly tight boundaries.

The Sahara is not and has never been the barrier to commerce trade or interaction among African people it has appeared to be to some writers. In fact, it is a culturally interactive arena itself and has been a greater context for such interaction in the past. Herodotus spoke of the Garamantes, whose capital now appears to have been Garama in the Libyan Desert as being a people who controlled areas of the vast desert. These people may have been related to the contemporary Tawerghans or most likely to the Toubou in central and southern Libya. But long before the Garamantes, indeed at least 10,000 years earlier, Africans whose physical features were like those of the Hausa and Yoruba built canals and villages in the desert. Thus, we cannot speak correctly of Africa north of the Sahara or south of the Sahara; the Sahara is Africa and numerous African people inhabit the Sahara.

The definition of society useful to our discussion is an interrelated set of habits created and maintained by humans interacting. As a point of reference culture is a cognitive concept about how humans interact, create, maintain, and develop institutions inasmuch as culture exists in the brain as well as in the execution. Although Christian Thomsen had divided prehistory into *stone, bronze,* and *iron* ages we now know that this division was too arbitrary. Societies did not all go through the same stages and if they did they went through them differentially. Furthermore, the great variety of human societies requires more flexible conceptual approaches for analysis. The imposition of concepts derived from

European analysis alone tends to obscure the fact that all current societies have been more or less successful.

CLASSIFICATORY ASPECTS OF AFRICOLOGY

Among Africologists the study of African phenomena is primarily an examination of *cultural/aesthetic, social/behavioral,* and *policy issues.* It is generally accepted that these three knowledge areas, judiciously studied, can be used to examine all phenomena. A growing literature in the field suggests that serious scholarship in economics or drama, history or politics, can be classified in one of the knowledge areas. Literatures are emerging around each of these cluster areas with direct interest to Africological issues.

CULTURAL/AESTHETIC

By the cluster term cultural/aesthetic is meant the creative, artistic, and inventive aspect of human phenomena that demonstrates the expression of values, arts, and the good. The beautiful is a sub-category of the good and is therefore not highlighted in this definition. To be good is to be beautiful according to an Afrocentric perspective.

We reserve the term cultural/aesthetic for most of what is usually called in the West the arts and humanities: music, dance, literature, history, philosophy, painting, and theater. What we study in this area are the significant elements in African phenomena, whether continental or Diasporan, that give meaning to cultural character. By cultural character is meant the essence of a people's history and icons in harmonious tension. Maulana Karenga has suggested seven constituents of culture: history, religion, motif, ethos, economic, political, and social organization.[6] *History* is the coherent record of the achievements of a people. *Religion* or mythology is the ritualized manner in which people present themselves to humanity. *Motif* represents the icons and symbols through which people announce themselves as human. *Ethos* is how you are projected to the world. Economic, political, and social organizations give legitimacy and power. Karenga found these concepts to be central to any discussion of culture.

On the other hand, Cheikh Anta Diop has advanced a conception of culture that includes three factors: psychic, historic, and linguistic. In his view as seen in the *Cultural Unity of Black Africa,* the psychic factor is a mental factor; the historic deals with phenomena; and the linguistic is concerned with languages. Diop's intention is to demonstrate the unity of African culture by examining these factors.[7] In order to capture Karenga's constituents while not losing sight of Diop's traditional factors I have integrated these as including the living or dead, relationship to the cosmos, and the relationship to self. It is the area normally covered in the American system by fields such as sociology, psychology, economics, political science, urban studies, religion, and anthropology among other fields. As it is expressed in our discussion of phenomena the social/behavioral cluster includes the critique of Eurocentric interpretations of African phenomena as well. Therefore, it is both an analysis and a criticism of the manner African social or behavioral data have been interpreted.

The criticism derives from the need to set the record straight. Indeed the idea found embedded in European thought, particularly in the seventeenth, eighteenth, nineteenth, and twentieth centuries that Africans were inferior socially and behaviorally has tainted most of what passes for social science in the West, definitionally and conceptually. Few have been able to escape Alexander Pope's dictum in the *Essay on Man* (1733) "some are, and must be, greater than the rest" and its implication for European contact and interpretation of that contact with the rest of the world.[8] Stephen Jay Gould argues in *The Mismeasure of Man* that biological determinism, the idea that those perceived to be on the bottom, are made of poor brains or bad genes, was a shared context of European and American thinking about racial ranking. In fact, Gould contends that while racial prejudice may be as old as recorded history, "its biological justification imposed the additional burden of intrinsic inferiority upon despised groups, and precluded redemption by conversion or assimilation."[9]

The publication of Charles Darwin's *The Origin of the Species* in 1859 and his subsequent thirteen years of publications devoted to expanding and applying his notion of natural selection, which can be shown persuasively to be an oxymoron, the combining of two contradictory terms without reducing the tension between them to form a new concept. Indeed, Darwin worked within the general anti-African canon while at the same time attempting to state a theory of evolution that was against the intellectual wisdom of the day. Thus, social and racial motivations operated in Darwin's work as a function of the European male's pain and the contemporary pain of the Western doctor who wants to deliver health care to an African American family who still insists on having a hoodoo priest present.

THE PROBLEMS OF METHOD

All methods of doing research have philosophical roots with specific assumptions about phenomena, human inquiry, and knowledge. The Africanist's frame of reference has too often been Eurocentric, that is, flowing from a conceptualization of African people developed to support the Western version of Africa. The problem exists because so much of the Western tradition is firmly grounded in Hegel's conception of history.[10] Hegel elaborated three histories or three ways of writing history: original, reflective, and philosophical. Original history, such as that of Herodotus and Thucydides, describes actions, events, and conditions that the historian saw with his own eyes or received reports of from others.

These primary historians are concerned with "what is actual and living in their environment." Such a history is a contemporary report of events and conditions. In Hegel's sense of original history certain sociologists or anthropologists might be said to be historians.

Reflective history may be universal, pragmatic, critical, or fragmentary. In its so-called "universal" form it seeks to survey an entire people, country, or the world. Hegel sees problems with this method of history, chief of which is the remarkable ability of some historians to not transfer their contemporary frame of mind to the period they are writing about at the moment. Thus, he describes a Livian history that makes Roman kings and generals speak in the manner of lawyers of the Livian era and not in the traditions of Roman antiquity.

The pragmatic form allows the historian to write about past events at a present time; the confluence of events and conditions, assist in nullifying the past, and therefore all periods of history, in spite of themselves, must decide within and in accordance with its own age. Fascinated by the idea of spirit, Hegel does not count reflective history valuable unless it is history committed to exploring the deep patterns of a people. Hegel's condemnation of German reflective histories is not that they did not follow the French example of creating a present for themselves and referring the past to the present condition.

Critical history is the evaluation of historical narratives and examples for their truth and trustworthiness. The key contribution of this method is in the ability of the author to extract results from narration rather than events. Although Hegel is content to isolate this form as a part of the reflective method of history he is critical of it as history. Historiography, for example, could not rightly be called history and higher criticism was itself suspect because of what Hegel sees as its "subjective fancies" replacing definite facts.

The fourth form of reflective history is fragmentary. Hegel writes that it is "abstractive but, in adopting universal points of view for example the history of art, of law, of religion—it forms a transition to philosophical world history." The aim of this kind of conceptual history is always to find the guide to the inner soul of a people. Hegel's metaphysics, the principal introduction of metaphysics for the Western world, comes out in his notions of guides of the soul, the idea is in truth, the spirit, rational, and necessary will. It is impossible to understand Hegel's concept of reflective history without knowing that for him history is really spirit performing in time as nature is idea in space.

The third Hegelian method of history is philosophical. He finds the need to justify this type of historical method because unlike the cases of the original and reflective histories the concept is not self-explanatory. The Hegelian concept of philosophical history is the thoughtful contemplation of history on the basis of data of reality. This he contrasts to philosophy that allegedly produces its own ideas out of speculation, without regard to given data.

Critics may assume that objectivity is compromised when the investigator uses the descriptive mode for Afrocentric research. The Afrocentrist is skeptical of the European concept of objectivity because it is invalid operationally. Marimba Ani is correct to evaluate the concept of "objectivity" negatively in her brilliant essay on European culture.[11] I have argued that what often passes for objectivity is a sort of collective European subjectivity. Therefore, it may not serve any useful purpose to speak of objectivity and subjectivity as this division is artificial in and of itself. The Afrocentricist speaks of research that is ultimately verifiable in the experiences of human beings, the final empirical authority. Of course, the methods of proof are founded upon the principles of fairness and openness. Both concepts are based in the idea of doing something that can be shown to be fair in its procedure and open in its application. What is unconscionable is the idea that when a person makes any decision that the decision is "objective"; every decision, even one's choice of software for her or his word processor, is human and consequently "subjective."

One cannot conduct an authentic debate on the political philosophies of Jefferson, Hume, or Locke without a discussion of their doctrines of racial supremacy, sexism, exploitation of other nationalities, colonialism and slavery. The genuine scholar must seek to assess the views of the political theorists in light of the cultural, racial class, and gender context. The point is, no field of human knowledge can be divorced from its author's involvement as a human being in a given context.

Some critics assume that the investigator may rely too much on her opinions in collecting data from a social context with which the investigator is familiar. The Afrocentric method proposes the dual-collection paradigm to deal with that problem particularly as it relates to what may be cross-cultural or cross-national research projects. This is important because in too many cases the Eurocentric method allows an individual researcher to conduct research alone. In many cases in Africa, graduate students from American and European universities conduct research in communities that they have little in common with and expect to be able to make sense out of without assistance. This is probably one of the biggest sins of the Eurocentric methods. These students assume they can insure "objectivity" and make some sense out of what they discover in African communities. If accurate results are obtained it is often by default and luck not because of some objective method.

Two directives are invoked whenever the Africological researcher seeks to make a cross-cultural or trans-racial study. (1) The use of two researchers to collect similar data, at least one of whom must be from the social or cultural context, and (2) the assessment of the data by two evaluators, at least one of whom must be from the social or cultural context. In addition to the use of the dual-collection model researchers using the descriptive approach will also employ triangulation of information and in-depth interviews.

The nomothetic model of experimental laboratory research insists that variable control and manipulation are able to assist in universal laws is highly questionable. "Universal" is again one of those Eurocentric terms that has little meaning in the real world. People live in societies and operate within cultures. The aim of the descriptive researcher has to be the in-depth knowledge of a socio-human context in order to be able to make some sense out of it, to appreciate it, to live in peace with it. In actuality, this is counter to the experimental framework that is based on the logic of prediction, war, and the market. What is the need for the universal idea, the control and manipulation of variables, the predictive ability of the researchers? Based on the war games model, the Eurocentric social scientists went to the boards and to computers to be able to predict human behavior under adverse circumstances. Particularly advertising interests have now used this model in market research, in order to sell more products to African and Asian nations. The Afrocentric method must have a different goal; it must find its reason to be in the harmonizing mission. This is an interactive model rather than a distant, sterile, abstract, isolated, and non-contact model. Rather this method finds its strength in the cooperative and integrative function of human experiences.

Edmund Husserl's *Ideas: General Introduction to Phenomenology* provoked discussion around the issue of methodology in European social sciences! Husserl's introduction of phenomenology was a major advance for the social sciences. In fact, taking many of his ideas from continental African philosophy, Husserl posited a holistic view rather than a detached, isolated, disparate, reality. The phenomenologist's search for essence by questioning all assumptions about reality is similar to the Afrocentricist's search for essence by questioning all assumptions about reality that are rooted in a particularistic view of the universe. The distortion of social reality by traditional Eurocentric scientific methods occurs because of allegiance to a set of false assumptions. This is true whether we call the outcome of this way of viewing reality *post-colonialism* or *orientalism.*

The Afrocentric method shares some of the perceptions of the so-called "ethnomethodology" but differs in both its philosophical base and its conceptualization. What it shares with ethnomethodology is the idea that reality is a process and that the discussion of normative patterns cannot be made intelligently unless the researcher understands the social context. What I have difficulty with is the Eurocentric foundation of Harold Garfinkel's view. Although Garfinkel argued correctly that researchers should not assume common meaning is shared, he incorrectly assumed that the structure that accounted for subjects' perceptions was above and beyond the contextual meaning of their particular culture.

But the principal problem with ethnomethodology is its Eurocentric bias. What is ethnomethodology conceptually but the white Western Eurocentric researcher saying to other white Western Eurocentric researchers "We ought to study these other people from their own contexts?" "Ethno" is derived from the medieval English "ethnic" and the Late Latin "ethica" which means "heathen." Since the Eurocentric writers did not initially include white people in their conceptualization one can only speculate that ethnomethodology, like ethnomusicology, was meant to study those who were not Europeans.

A DIFFERENT VIEW

Our methodology must be holistic and integrative; our epistemology, participatory and committed. The Africologist is a working scholar committed to the advancement of knowledge about the African world. In pursuing a vision in Afrocentric scholarship the Africologist gathers facts about African phenomena, verifies them and subjects the interpretations to the strictest measures. The aim of the Africologist is to make the world more meaningful to those who live in it and to create spaces for human understanding. Our task is not like that of the Western social scientist who seeks to predict human behavior in order to advance more direct control over nature but rather to explain human nature as it is manifest in the African arena. All statements about objects, phenomena, and events are subjects for discussion, analysis, and action. To be a good Africologist, the scholar must be able to distinguish between Afrocentric statements and less precise non-Afrocentric statements. In fact, we can say this is the first qualification for a researcher.

The following statements, with their obvious biases, are found in contemporary Eurocentric scholarly works.

Kenneth Clarke once wrote:

> ... the Apollo embodies a higher state of civilization than the mask. They both represent spirits, messengers from another world.... To the negro imagination it is a world of fear and darkness, ready to inflict horrible punishment for the smallest infringement of a taboo to the Hellenistic imagination it is a world of light and confidence in which gods are like ourselves, only more beautiful,

and descend to earth in order to teach men reason and the laws of harmony.

Adriano Rodrigues also wrote:

They were forced to subjugate numbers of still primitive peoples as well as more civilized states. Two empires, both of which had reached a fairly high level of civilization, disappeared when the Spaniards arrived; the empire of the Aztecs in Mexico and that of the Incas in Peru.

In these two typical statements by Eurocentric writers one senses the bias against other cultures. Kenneth Clarke, well respected as a major force in European culture, demonstrates his prejudice against African culture and his ignorance of African art. He chooses to compare the Apollo with the mask, any mask, rather than to compare the Apollo with the Ramses at Abu Simbel or some similar sculpture from African classical antiquity. His contrast of a world of fear and a world of confidence represents self-conscious attempts to valorize the European experience above the African. The fact is that anyone capable of manipulating language could play the same game. One surely would not compare Stonehenge with the Giza Pyramids. Adriano Rodrigues' statement places his prejudices not so much in *comparisons* as in *omissions*, if certain things had been stated, they would have shown Spanish destruction of other civilizations. For example, Rodrigues says the Spaniards *"were forced to subjugate"* as if some divine force caused them to attack the people of the country. Furthermore, the indigenous civilizations are said to have *"disappeared"* when in fact someone *disappeared* them. We must also examine the nature of the mythic, epic expression. For example, the European writer Hegel finds a "firm individuality" as the only basis for history that on the surface seems so foreign to an African conception of community and history.

This is fundamentally unacceptable to the Africologist. It is because of such formulations that the meeting of the missionary David Livingston and mercenary Henry Morton Stanley in the African forest becomes history while hundreds of thousands of people living in the same time and space are said to be without history. An intellectual dishonesty, perpetrated by racist historians, allows history to be what happened to two Europeans in the midst of hundreds of thousands of Africans. Situated in the Neckar River Valley, separated from the wider world Hegel, and later Karl Jaspers, Jurgen Habermas and Hannah Arendt spent time contemplating the relationship of Germans and their culture to the rest of the world from their perch at Heidelberg University. Hegel, in particular, looked out from the philosopher's path and wrote nonsense about African people and African history. In Hegelian terms Africans are an obscure people, obscure in this instance because Europeans do not know them but certainly not obscure to their own recorders, musicians, historians, epics, myths, and chronicles. We cannot deny individual narratives but they must be placed within the context of the collective.

Hegel's position on Greece is like that of other European and American writers, indeed they view the Greek experience as a virgin birth of their own experience; of course, in numerous forms what has paraded as Greece derived is actually African derived. Hegel's predicament is even more complex because in philosophy he demonstrates an awesome ignorance of ancient African civilizations placing Egypt, even at this time, at the bottom of world civilizations. This was principally a Eurocentric reaction to an African civilization and since Hegel did have the benefit of reading the work of the French writers and scholars who wrote of the monumental nature of an African civilization, he could admit, with reluctance, the anteriority of Egypt, but he would not admit, even reluctantly, that Egypt was a high culture.

Furthermore, he is definite in his opinions about the supremacy of the Germanic people: "Only the Germanic peoples came, through Christianity, to realize that man as man is free and that freedom of Spirit is the very essence of man's nature." Inherent in Hegel's view of human nature and the role of world spirit in human matters is the belief that there is always "a dominant people" in whose history is the unfolding of the dominant phase of any epoch. The characteristics of Hegel's ethnocentric mind are seen in his presentation of the four historical worlds: Oriental, Greek, Roman, and German. He argues, in effect, that the rest of the world serves as an audience for the central position of each of these cultures. I am not the first to point to Hegel's arrogantly Eurocentric view of history. In fact, this aggressively European view has been re-set in Samuel Huntington's *The Clash of Civilizations* and in Samuel Howe's *Empire*. To some degree it was attempted without much success in Mary Lefkowitz's *Not Out of Africa* because of the push-back from black and other scholars. Their aim, it seems, is to shore up what they see as the multiplicity of challenges to a Western domination of ideas, concepts, and realities. As children of Hegel they are attempting to strengthen walls that have already begun to decay in the midst of the renaissance of Africa and other parts of the world.

The key to an adequate analysis of Hegel's posture on history is his prosecution of an ethnocentric perspective as if it were universal. To claim, as he did, that Africa, the birthplace of human civilizations, was devoid of morality and consequently ahistorical, was to demonstrate both an aggressive Eurocentrism and an ignorance of Africa. Granted that at the time of Hegel's first lectures Europeans did not understand the full significance of the African continent in the evolution of human society and paleontology; however, the lack of humility in the face of this ignorance is without defense.

THE HEGELIAN AFRICA

To prosecute the maligning of Africa it was necessary for Hegel to advance a false division of the continent, a division superimposed on the land, not by the people of the continent themselves, but by European historians, anthropologists, and colonial administrators who said Africa consisted of Asian Africa, European Africa, and Africa proper. In *Philosophy of History* he explained that Africa proper was the territory south of the Sahara; European Africa was the territory north of the Sahara; Egypt was the part of Africa connected to Asia. This division is arbitrary and has no validity in point of fact. Africa is geographically and culturally, due to natural barriers, more continental than Europe. There is neither an Africa north of the Sahara nor south of the Sahara as Hegel claimed; the Sahara is Africa and human populations have inhabited the Sahara for thousands of years. It is as useless to speak of Africa separated by deserts, as it is to speak of separations by rain forests. What Hegel and others of his school of thought have attempted to argue since the emergence of the Aryan model is that Africa in its northern areas was somehow different qualitatively from Africa in the southern areas. This is why Hegel could say of Africa that it was "a land of childhood, which lying beyond the day of self-conscious history, is enveloped in the dark mantle of night." Such commentary shows an extreme disregard for the historical processes carried out by Africans in various cultural and social contexts for many millennia. Indeed, Egypt, the grandest civilization of antiquity, was necessarily seen in Hegel's view as belonging more to Arabic influences than African, despite the fact that African civilization in Egypt had flourished 4,000 years prior to the coming of the Arabs.

Hegel must have been aware of the contradictory bases of his discussion of African geography. One cannot assert the continental definition of Africa geographically while trying to deny Africa's unity culturally by insisting that the "real Africa" is actually only a portion of the continent. European Africa, of course, never existed and was merely the Hegelian attempt to Germanicize all of those people who may have contributed to African coastal civilizations. Hegel's claims for northern Africa being European or Asian are no more to be accepted or believed than someone else's claims that southern Europe was actually African Europe. Cheikh Anta Diop is most authoritative on this question, contending that a black African people occupied the northern part of the African continent since "prehistoric" times."

As to Egypt being connected to Asia, as Hegel claims without any evidence, Diop is most clear:

> ...if a civilization comparable to that of Egypt had flowered there [in Asia] ... its memory, no matter how vague, would have been transmitted to us by the Ancients, who form one branch of the Indo-Europeans, who furnished so many corroborative testimonials on the Negro-Egyptian culture.[12]

What is more certain, however, is the intimate connection of ancient Egypt with Nubia, Punt, Libya, and Ethiopia. Since the Nile River is the principal organ of Egyptian social, historical, civic and monumental life, is not it natural that the civilizations of the Nile Valley would be more closely related to ancient Egypt than more distant and less accessible lands?

Perhaps one of the most revealing statements in the *Philosophy of History* is Hegel's assurance that "among the Negroes moral sentiments are quite weak, or more strictly speaking, nonexistent." Such rhetoric was probably not unusual as the spirit of the time in Europe was one of racial expansionism and growing sentiments for the doctrine of Germanic racial supremacy. Morality would prove in both the nineteenth and twentieth centuries not to be a special attribute reserved for Germanic peoples.

Hegel's place in Eurocentrism is supreme and next to Plato he is the most influential thinker in the European pantheon. But his speculative idealism in historical thinking has led to some permutations that have entrapped the best minds of Europe and America. Without a doubt Hegel's influence on sociology, history, political science, and philosophy remains prominent and insidious. Its prominence is seen in the quotations, allusions, and examples taken from his works by contemporary scholars; his insidiousness is found in the structure of thought found in the writings of European and American scholars. While it is true that Hegel's ideas on the Absolute, the world spirit, dialectics, and ethical idealism provoked some reaction in the works of the Marxists, Kierkegaard, G. E. Moore, and others, he nevertheless was seldom checked by his European critics or followers for his racist views regarding Africans or Asians. Furthermore, the works of Theodor Adorno and Herbert Marcuse, although rooted in Hegelian ideas and used for quite different purposes than Hegel may have appreciated, are valuable for their endeavor to forge new relevance out of Hegel's dialectic. Yet clearly the Hegelian philosophy was responsible for the historicist crisis that led to Marx and Kierkegaard as opposed to a Goethean serenity based on the eternal return motif. Historicism itself owes a large debt to Hegel's influence. But historicism has raised numerous questions among philosophers and the ensuing debates have thrown light on the nature of the European anxiety over method. In many ways, this is a good thing because as Yoshitaka Miike has shown the idea of rationality itself, as presented by Hegelians and others, is often misleading in a discourse about world knowledge.[13]

HISTORICISM AND THE DEBATE OVER KNOWLEDGE

Karl Popper's attack on historicism, the ideology of laws of history and development, has been answered in part by the work of Michel Foucault and Thomas Kuhn in the prosecution of their view that systems of thought are essentially the products of rules. Of course, these rules are often unclear to the practitioners of the systems and only become evident to those who retrospectively reflect on the meaning of social development, human nature, or social relations.

My concern is that this debate deepens rather than eliminates the errors inherent in an overreaching domestic squabble within Eurocentric intellectual circles. There can be no either-or positions that are taken on every issue and in science, philosophy, history, and sociology. In one thing Popper is correct and that is the poverty of historicism that has given birth to pernicious and rigid doctrines that endanger human freedom.[14] In fact, as an Afrocentrist it is clear to me that there has been an overreach of rationality in the West as well. What we have seen with the end of rationality is the Holocaust, the creation of apartheid in South Africa, the dropping of murderous atomic bombs on Hiroshima and Nagasaki, the murder of Bosnian Muslims in Sbrenica, the genocide of the Tutsis in Rwanda, the ethnic cleansing of the Darfurians by the Islamic Khartoum regime, the Christian American building of concrete and steel walls between human beings, and other rational acts! Beyond this, however, is the matter of strict systems of thought that engender either-or positions. The real poverty exists in the tradition that pits historicism against ahistoricism, structuralism against deconstruction, men against women, white against black, etc. These are illusions built into our response patterns by the contemporary emphasis on either-or situations.

Paul Feyerabend recognizes the illusionary status of any kind of framework and claims that anarchy must replace rationalism in the theory of knowledge. His position, supported by a growing number of converts, is that intellectual progress can only be achieved by stressing creativity, wishes, and intuitions rather than the method and authority of science. While I submit that Feyerabend has advanced Western thought in regards to knowledge, one must not misunderstand the nature of his significant enterprise in a world context. The Afrocentrist has never abandoned the position that knowledge must be sought in every human encounter with self, nature and the cosmos. Thus, *Against Method* simply rejects the rationalist merry-go-round and argues for the "withering away of reason" because "the only principle which does not inhibit progress is anything goes."[15] On one hand, the differences between Popper and Feyerabend are significant; on another, the notion of framework creates anxiety equally in both. To a large degree, their concerns have found articulation in Sartre's existentialism that sees society as absurd, cruel, and without mercy on the poor lonely individual. Feyerabend particularly rushes to disavow allegiance to any method and perhaps his clarity has allowed him to abandon this notion of rationality as good; this is a good thing.

To the contrary, Africology advances on all fronts simultaneously. It does not deny rationalism its historical place but neither does it deny other forms of human inquiry their places in the acquisition of knowledge. The human being can reason without lessons in logic and can learn without being instructed. To advance knowledge the fundamental ingredients have to be openness to all possibilities, freedom of thought, evaluation of all data received by the human person, and the integration of all methods advanced by human beings into the intellectual inquiry. Methods of history, literary criticism, history of science, botany, economics, zoology, biology, politics, medicine, and law are not necessarily contradictory and cannot be dismissed as unimportant in the search for understanding of the human condition. This is the way

African sciences proceeded prior to the Greek assertion advanced by the Germanic school. Wholesale construction of pyramids throughout the African continent and other large-scale projects were carried out with combinations of ideas, tasks, and actions. This is why it is possible to claim that the African pyramid age was the first human university where all the acquired knowledge of humanity was used in the grand constructions.

What appeared later, much later, as European sciences must be criticized, however, for their exclusion of the "other," for their construction of an either-or paradigm, and for their antifeminist posture. Thus, in the context of Africology most of the European-derived sciences and arts treat Africans and African contributions as irrelevant to knowledge acquisition. Such arrogance stands at the door to most fields of European studies. Any examination of religion, for example, will show that few American or European books on religion actually give as much weight to African religion as to Judaism, Christianity, Islam, Hinduism, and Buddhism. This is the case although Africans were the first people recorded to have a concept of religion. No other people named the "gods" before Africans! Who called the names Ptah, Ra, Atum, and Amen, as Almighty before Africans? Furthermore, at least one African religion, Yoruba, has grown into an international religion with more than 100 million adherents.

One must often use different sensibilities to gain access to knowledge; these sensibilities give Afrocentric methods greater absorption capacities. If we examine history, we must also discard some of the traditional patterns of asking questions to obtain knowledge. Therefore, to determine how the hospitality shown to Europeans by members of King Ansah's Fante royal family in Ghana in 1482 was misunderstood, the scholar applies a multiplicity of methods while maintaining the essential core Afrocentric perspective.

In reality, this means looking at the encounter from the standpoint of the Fante rather than the Portuguese—the relatively undiscussed as opposed to the more discussed—through examination of oral traditions, linguistics, material transformation, court practices in Fante, external trade patterns as a result of the encounter, legends, myths, or any rumors found among non-Fante peoples. The Africologist advances beyond the mechanistic moment and grasps the dynamic and rhythmic process by which we live-in-the world. This living-in-the-world becomes the ground in which we find authentic empiricism. In this respect Afrocentric inquiry is both particular and general inquiry. It is particular inquiry in the sense that it engages the scholar creatively as a person who lives in the world; it is general because it operates as social inquiry encompassing psychological, cultural, and mythical dimensions of human life, thereby superseding the mechanistic model with its rather static profile.

Trained in Eurocentric perspectives most contemporary scholars have only seen from a Eurocentric viewpoint and this view is decidedly different from that of the African person who has been victimized by the imposition of Eurocentric expression. Afrocentricity is inevitably the philosophy of African scholarship in this historical moment. One cannot transcend it until it has been exhausted in its confrontation with our reality. The circumstances, the set of circumstances are uniquely social, but it is only out of the social environment that one is able to derive the authentic empirical experience, otherwise we are playing head games.

The failure of the Africanists to make any real gains against the dominant and dominating white and Western ethos that is at the base of so many of Africa's problems is precisely due to the predicament of contradiction. These Africanists, whether black or as is most often the case, white, are trapped in theoretical and methodological prisons from which they can only escape with great danger to their reputations. Since they are participating in a Western enterprise and seek the accoutrements that come with that enterprise they must add to the store of theory or method that builds that enterprise no matter what the area of study. Thus for the Africanist who studies the economy of Kenya, the aim is to add to economic theory and method, a Western enterprise, more than to add to the liberation of the African nation's economy from the grip of the West. The same can be said about the historian, anthropologist, and linguist; only the Afrocentric scholar rises to a new level of consciousness which claims that it is the concrete act of turning the table so that Africa assumes centrality that grants

African people a new economic, historical or linguistic vision. Indeed, we make the future by virtue of realizing in our actions the predominant objective task for restructuring the present. The authentic empirical experience is living-in-the-world with an appreciation of the individual as the motive force for social reconstruction. Afrocentric method approaches all African phenomena from the standpoint of African centrality. Naturally this centrality cannot be left to chance, it must respond to a theoretical framework where each phenomenon is examined within the context of the authentic empiricism so fundamental to the methodology.

The leap of imagination one finds in the best Afrocentric scholars gets its energy from the African aesthetic sensibility. What one seeks in a study is the merger of facts with beauty; this becomes the creative quest for interpretation that "looks good" while it is explaining. Any time a scholar reaches a dead end in interpretation or analysis it is usually because he or she is utilizing the traditional methods. New discoveries will be made in authentically new ways on the edge of risk. Such studies will undoubtedly receive grudging admiration at first but they represent the only exit from a Eurocentric, male dominated view of the world. We are led to the Afrocentric idea of holism, everything is everything, and we are a part of the one and the other is our own measure. To begin this pilgrimage towards disentanglement will mean that we must find intellectual paths that have long been covered by the superimposition of mono-ethnic ideas as universal.

C. Tsehloane Keto wrote in his provocative historiography, *The Africa Centered Perspective of History,* that "different regions of the world that have evolved distinct cultures are entitled to develop paradigms based on the perspectives of the region's qualitatively significant human cultures, histories and experiences."[16] I would say that they are not only "entitled" but that they actually create out of their own cultural contexts. Keto believes that a perspective called "pluriversal" can only occur by "extrapolating global rather than regional trends." Indeed, Keto believes that "the trouble at present is that studies about the rest of the world are overly influenced and often distorted by theories and conclusions drawn from studies based on a minority of the world's families, a minority of the world's women, a minority of the world's social structures and a minority of the world's cultures."[17]

The insights of scholars such as Keto provide the basis for Africological theories. Here the work of Lucius Outlaw must be considered in the philosophical context of the emergence of Africology. In fact, in his seminal 1987 paper "Africology: Normative Theory", Lucius Outlaw explains the necessity of rules governing a discipline. He says, "the rules—the norms—for obtaining such agreement are not provided by melanin."[18] Outlaw underscores the position I have taken when discussing Afrocentricity because it is not simply a race-based theory of any kind; it is fundamentally about cultural agency. As a theory it is not, nor can it be based on biological determinism. Anyone willing to submit to the discipline of learning the concepts and methods may acquire the knowledge necessary for analysis.

In a sense, a revolution has already begun. Led by a host of Kemetic scholars of African origin and with the participation of several European scholars, the movement toward decolonizing information and approaches to information has touched ancient chronology, classificatory studies of civilization, African American literary studies, resistance activities of colonized and enslaved peoples, and the structure of knowledge itself. It is particularly important for us to advance a more reasonable chronology and real perspective of ancient Egypt.

CHAPTER TWO

A Mobilization of Ideas

The paradigm of Afrocentricity is an advance that adds to an Afrocentric construction of time periods. Indeed, Brooks makes his case on the basis of rainfall records in the Sahel and Sahara regions. For some eight millennia, from ca. 18000 until ca. 10000 B.C., while Europe and North America experienced the last period of extensive glaciation, the northern part of the African continent sustained extremely arid conditions. By using the period 1930-1960 as a base period for determining rainfall and aridity in the Sahara (during the base period the annual rainfall was approximately 100 mm), Brooks showed that between 9000-6000 B.C. there were "populations inhabiting the Sahara area and a wide belt of territory extending southwards along the upper Nile Valley and into the Lakes region of East Africa [which] shared a way of life that J. E. G. Sutton has characterized as the Aquatic Civilization of Middle Africa."[1] Brooks' periodization attempts to use an African-centered basis for establishing the chronology of Africa. If one looks at the rise of civilization in the northeastern corner of the continent one sees that the Kemetic people's rise is nearly parallel with the time markers one finds in the western part of the continent, particularly in relationship to the trading villages along the Niger River bend. Documentation of the Niger River bend civilizations is not as extensive at the present time as that in the Nile Valley.

The Ascendance of Kemetic Periods: The first extensively documented people to occupy Kemet, the land now known as Egypt were the Badarians, a black African people who are authoritatively dated to 6,000 B.C. Although San and Twa types are said to go back to 30,000 B.C., evidences of their presence are largely found in the desert rock paintings rather than everyday artifacts such as pottery and hunting implements. On the other hand, the Badarians left a strong record of material evidences and their morphological character also is well established. The usual period classification of Kemetic history consists of two chronological phases: (1) predynastic and (2) dynastic. The predynastic phase is imprecise in its origin. I have chosen therefore to speak of the remote predynastic and the near predynastic. The *remote predynastic* is from the initial human occupation of Kemet to the Badarian age.

The *near predynastic* is from the Badarian period to the uniting of the two lands by Menes the Great. The near predynastic period can be divided into the Badarian, Amratean, and Gerzean ages. Establishing the Badarian morphological character is necessary to counter what Davidson, Bernal, Karenga, and Carruthers have seen as the anti-African positions taken by European scholars during the nineteenth century.[2] European scholars, following Hegel, insisted that Africans developed no civilizations, even those on the African continent. Therefore, they showed antipathy to the idea that the first Egyptians were, in fact, black. This is one of the reasons the Afrocentrists have had to return to the earliest documents written by Greeks and others to determine the written evidence. Of course, the Egyptians were quite clear themselves in the portrayals of their populations. In my book, *Herodotus on Egypt* (2013), I once again translated and presented Herodotus' own statement on the question of the color of the ancient Egyptians. It is clear that the ancient Egyptians had black skin and wooly hair from the observation of this Greek writer of the 5th century BC. The farther back one goes the blacker the ancient Egyptians are; knowing Egypt since the conquests is not the same as understanding its culture and people from the dawn of Kemetic history.[3]

THE MORPHOLOGICAL CHARACTER

Most previous work examining the morphology of the Badarians, even when attempting to present a constructive thesis, has been flawed with a Eurocentric bias. For example, Eugen Strouhal's article on the Badarian morphology question is entitled "Evidence of the Early Penetration of Negroes into Predynastic Egypt."[4] Such a title assumes that "negroes" is a scientific term and that the indigenous people of Kemet were not Africans (blacks). The so-called "negroes" did not have to penetrate Egypt because the people of Kemet had "black skin and wooly hair." Thus, even the Europeans who attempted to demonstrate a black presence in Egypt did so from the unscientific and racist premise that it was somehow exceptional that Africans occupied Africa. Strouhal's work, although published in the 1970s, is a direct theoretical descendant of what Bernal has called the Aryan model even though it is not Strouhal's intention to support that model. In effect, the negation of the model takes the model as reference point and is thereby as Eurocentric as the model itself. My own analysis of Strouhal's work suggests an over-eager attempt to support an unsubstantiated thesis regarding ancient Egypt when most reputable scholars had abandoned the thesis as unsupported by the evidence. Strouhal's work is flawed in respect to the racial question. If one looks at the Badarians from the standpoint of German race theory where races were to constitute certain uniform characteristics rather than as gene pools that perhaps yield similar characteristics, it is possible to see how Strouhal could classify the 117 Badarian skulls he examined as being comprised of ninety-four mixed Negroid-Europoid, eight purely Negroid, and fifteen Europoid samples.

Strouhal, however, is immediately in a quandary with the thesis he seeks to uphold. One could just as easily say that the 117 Badarian skulls he examined showed 102 were clearly Africoid while only fifteen showed any possibility of being related in morphology to Europoids. Furthermore, he admits that his examination included only the available Badarian skulls located in the Duckworth Laboratory at Cambridge (fifty-three skulls) and the Institute of Anatomy at Kasr El-Aini University of Cairo (sixty-four skulls). Of course, this means that it is very difficult to draw any other conclusion about the morphology of the Badarians other than that in the limited sample they were overwhelmingly Africoid. Strouhal's opening sentence contains all of the explosives that have surrounded classical African civilizations since the French invasions of the Nile Valley. Strouhal writes, "Theories about the Negro origin of the Ancient Egyptians have been with Egyptology ever since its beginnings."[5] Basing most of their early work on cranial theories, these Aryan modelers undertook to determine if Africans could truly have built the ancient civilizations of the Nile. Both Nubia and Kemet (Egypt) became the object of these craniometrists as they studied nasal and alveolar profile angles, nasal indices, indices of the *ramus mandibulae*, indices of the prominence of the nasal root (the height of the nasal root above the level of the anterior inter-orbital breadth), shape of the foreheads, nasal spines, and prominence of cheekbones. Such was the frantic search to demonstrate that although Africans were prominent in the Nile Valley civilizations, they must have migrated there from some other place!

In the face of Stouhal's questions about origin, Cheikh Anta Diop showed that the naturalistic statue of a woman made of ivory and discovered during the first excavation period (tomb 5107) was clearly African by examining her relatively broad nose and demonstrating that the example was similar to many ordinary Africans in Senegal and elsewhere. Anthony Browder, one of the most serious African American excavators of the Nile Valley Civilization, has through his foundation, ASA Restoration Project, reported on the blackness of Karakhamun, a 25th Dynasty priest whose tomb was found in South Asasif area of the West Bank.[6] Dr. Elena Pischikova, the leader of the expedition said that the tomb of priest Karakhamun was discovered in the 19th century but never excavated and continued to deteriorate and was not fully accessible until Pischikova, with the financial and excavating assistance of Browder and his crews, rediscovered the tomb and began the process of conservation.[7]

Neither Strouhal nor the more strident contemporary anti-African origin of civilization scholars can make any sense out of their positions. They want to say that the classical civilizations of the Nile Valley were not possible without European input. Thus, Mary Lefkowitz, whom I debated four times, has written a very deceptive work called *Not Out of Africa*.[8] It was this book that prompted my work, *The Painful Demise of Eurocentrism*.[9] In the end, however, the argument loses ground on several counts. In the first place, when the Badarians settled in Kemet there was neither a Europe nor any knowledge of what a European was or was to become. There were, on the other hand, people of the continent of Africa. The Badarians, living on the continent, were clearly Africans. The people are called Badarians after the village of Badari in southern Egypt where flint instruments, pottery, and other material evidences of one of the earliest African civilizations were found. In the second place, Cheikh Anta Diop has proven conclusively that foreign elements in the Nile Valley were intruders, mainly from Asia. Indeed, the beauty and elegance of Diop's work is that even if we walked a path backwards we would run into his arguments proving that the African people of the Nile Valley were black and that all other populations who were not black would have become black in a short time. These people, intruders, were often absorbed into the indigenous African population. Europeans are not present in any significant numbers prior to the 4th century B.C. Thus, the Badarians, who first appeared in the 4th millennia, were indigenous Africans.

G. Brunton and G. Caton-Thompson reconstructed many details of Badarian life. They contend that belief in the after-life first appears in Badarian ideology.[10] Strouhal says that nose-rings and earrings appear to be of African origin because of the presence of such decorative jewelry pieces in the grave-sites.[11] Other ideas attributed to the Badarians include astral and celestial worship, and ritual killing of the king in times of his decreased strength. Unquestionably, the basis of the religious, social, and decorative beliefs and practices of ancient Kemet are found in the early practices of the Badarians, who incidentally are everywhere acknowledged as an African, black civilization.

KEMET AND THE GREAT LAKES OF AFRICA: A NEW SCIENTIFIC EVALUATION

One of the advantages for Afrocentrists and other scholars of ancient Kemet has been the incomparable work of Cheikh Anta Diop. He covered more areas of possible connections between ancient Kemet and other parts of the African continent than any one else. In *Civilization or Barbarism* and in *The African Origin of Civilization* he laid out the plan for solid Afrocentric scholarship in the area of African history. However, it was in his linguistic and scientific studies, including his melanin studies, that he advanced the study of the field and opened the possibilities for new scholarship.

As recent as 2012 and 2013 new evidence has been demonstrated further linking the Nile Valley civilization of ancient Kemet to the Nile civilization of the Great Lakes Region of Africa and points south. Scientists have examined the DNA of a several mummies taken from the Amarna Period during the latter half of the 18ᵗʰ Dynasty and part of the 19ᵗʰ Dynasty, the Ramessid Period, to determine their relationship to other Africans. This was the period when the royal palace was moved to Akhetaten called "Horizon of the Aten" when Akhenaten who changed his name from Amenhotep IV disagreed with the priests of Waset and exalted Aten above all the other deities of the land. Reigning from 1353 to 1336 Akhenaten literally shifted the entire cosmology of the ruling family. It would take Akhenaten's successors to restore the historic order and harmony in the religious sphere of the society. Later, during the period of the Ramsesses the nation of Kemet would become one of the greatest empires of the ancient world. Thus, the mummies examined came from these periods in Egypt's past.

Matching the DNA profiles of people from the Great Lakes region of Uganda with that of the Amarna and Ramessid Period mummies scientists have concluded that the per-aas (pharaohs) of ancient Egypt were related to the Ugandan people. In December 2012 tests on Ramses III and his son showed that they belonged to the Y-Chromosome group Elbla. This the same group as Africans who speak the so-called Niger-Congo languages. Of course, this caused some consternation among European scholars who had argued for a white Egypt and therefore other DNA studies were made by a company called DNA Tribes in 2013. The result was that the mummies autosomal profiles turned out to be the same as that of present day populations of Africans in the Great Lakes Region and Southern Africa that means that they were basically the same humans. This evidence was reported in the DNA

Tribe's digest in February 1, 2013. The report says, "Among present day world populations, Ramesses III's autosomal STR profile is most frequent in the African Great Lakes Region where it is approximately 335.1 times as frequent as it is in the world as a whole."[12] It also said that the Egyptian royal mummies matched the results of the present day populations in Africa. Beyond this, however, was the ceremonial and material evidences that showed the connection between ancient Kemet and the Great Lakes region of Africa. Among the many similarities are female co-heirs, use of royal drums and twin objects on solemn occasions in contemplation of societal wellbeing, the king's shooting of arrows in four directions as symbolic of the willingness of the king to defend the empire, the playing of bow-harps and flutes, and the use of canoes held together with vegetative materials similar to those of ancient Egypt.

In fact, we now know from Spencer Wells's projects and those of other scholars that the peopling of Europe and Asia was the direct result of African migration to those continents, a migration that occurred long before the development of Badarian civilization. As Wells sees it, all humans alive today are descended from a single African man who lived around 60,000 – 90,000 years ago.[13] This means that the oldest civilizations that we can think of owe their origins to Africa. How ironic that those who are often the loudest in attacking Africa and Africans are the youngest children of the continent?

THE KEMETIC LEGACY

The foundation of all African speculation in religion, art, ethics, moral customs, and aesthetics are derived from systems of knowledge found in ancient Egypt. To some extent it is this African foundation, rather than the Greeks, that has made a lasting impact on the Western world although some challenge this position, especially when they want to argue that Europe is an exceptional culture.

EGYPTIAN CONCEPTS IN OTHER AFRICAN SOCIETIES

We readily understand how Greek, for instance, has informed English with words like: meteorology, biography, biology, geology, aeronautics, astronomy, tragedy, comedy, elegiac, didactic, gramophone, drama, idea, theory, practice, philosophy, and ethical. Indeed, it would be difficult to discuss anything of significance in English without some deference to Greek.

The debt owed to classical ciKam, the language of Kemet, by other African societies is as extensive as the debt owed to Greek in some Western societies. Since the work in this area is only now beginning to be done linguistically we will rely almost entirely on the understanding of deeper and subtler meanings of ritual concept. Where it may not now be possible to establish a one-to-one correlation in a particular language with ciKam, we are able to show concept similarity. Behind such similarity, of course, is the term or word that often remains undiscovered. Now that African scholars have begun to investigate their own interconnections through language we have seen an enormous leap in concept similarity, for example, the continuing use of "Tut" or "Djehuti" as a name among the Nuer much like the ancient Kemites used it in Tutankhamen. The word "tutu" appears in numerous widely dispersed African languages and contexts and has a direct relationship to ancient ciKam.

There are cases, however, where an African word from ciKam, e.g., "hbny," *ebony*, occurs in other African languages as well as European languages either as a borrowed word or an invading word coming on the heels of soldiers. Such was the significance of the classical African language that certain expressions leaped from the African continent to Europe at an early stage.

The Kemetic heritage penetrates the literature, the orature, the pottery, the burial rituals, the procreative myths, and the modes of thought of Africa. It is the classical African civilizations themselves that have given us so much organic contact with the history of ideas. The vivid example of the massive memorials to African genius such as *Ipet Isut* at the temple now called Karnak, the temples and tombs of the Valley of the Kings, the Pyramids, the major shrines, resonates with what we now know about the rest of the continent. When we feel, even now, the rhythms of creation in dance, art, literature, music, and talk the African intimacy with nature and fullness with life, we are experiencing our own standards, values, and codes exhibited in our approach to life thousands of years later. The festivals, the color, the vibrancy, the appeal to the deities, the incessant discussion, the dance, movement, show us ourselves dancing with the gods along the banks of the Nile.

During thousands of years of history prior to its struggle with outside influences, Kemet shaped and molded its distinctive mode of African civilization. It contrasted sharply with the crude customs of northern barbarians and the incipient cultures of the East. Kemet was pre-eminent in art, literature, astronomy, medicine, divination, geometry, and ethics—all roads actually led to Kemet. The achievements of Kemetic genius are found in the civilizing role it played in Africa and the world. The Kemetic people seemed to reason about every aspect of human activity. They did not lose themselves in wonderment nor in idle self-congratulation but in intellectual and artistic pursuits that would govern human ideas for many centuries. If we were to state explicitly our debt to Kemet, we would have to say they gave us a sense of the possible. We owe to them the basis of science, art, ethical teachings, religion, dance, monarchy, and ritual drama. It is at the feet of Kemet that all civilizations in antiquity had to sit and admire what the black men and women had constructed along the Nile. Today the great descendants of these early Nile Valley peoples, Nubians, Darfurians, Dinka, Nuer, Shilluk, Uduk, and one hundred more ethnic groups are resurrecting their quest for liberation from the clutches of an alien culture.

I do not contend that Kemet was perfect, as some have claimed of ancient Greece, but there is no question that it was anterior in the design of the just and beautiful as reflected in ciKam itself. There is no "mysterious perfection" in Kemetic architecture, writing, and art but rather the majestic combination of soul and beauty that produced the standards of the sublime by which the world would follow. In ethical teachings as in art and science, we find that the works of the ancient Kemetic people are foundational for other cultures. In Arabic, for example, we find derivations from the ancient Kemetic language:

Kemetic	Arabic
Atum	Adam
Set	Satan
Hathor	Hajar
Ma'at	Ma'ad
Amen	Amin
Ausar	Asar

One might contrast the younger Greek art with Kemet by saying that whereas realism, lines, and symmetry became the central principles of Greek art, Kemetic art introduced measure, color, and right ordering of symbols as the premises for perfection. One sees this explicitly in the glyphs, the elemental level of the Kemetic mind's rendering of the beautiful. No society had ever paid more attention to the positioning of symbols and size of icons for aesthetic effect. What Kemet established remains the standard by which the African world and numerous other societies evaluate their artistic productions. Balance, timing, rhythm (right ordering), and color contrast are significant criteria for evaluation. Compared to Kemetic art and architecture, Greek expressions are simpler, less majestic, more austere, that is, as the European thinkers would say, spare.

It is no accident that with the conquest of Kemet by Alexander the Greek in 333 BC that the methods of Kemet passed to the Greeks. Consequently, the names of the sciences in most Western languages are now Greek names: mathematics, psychology, philosophy, biology, sociology, theology, meteorology, zoology, physics, and physiology. This is the case although Africans made the first advances in the older sciences, named the stars in the sky, called the days of the week, and studied the nature and rhythm of planting and harvest. Clearly philosophy was the most African of all of the early sciences, but it was not conceived of as Europe would conceive it as simply rational thinking. Indeed, the notion in African thought was always about wisdom. With Greek conquest came not only the subjugation of territory and people; but also the expropriation of ideas, concepts, and sciences. Herodotus says clearly that: "The names of nearly all of the gods came from Egypt to Greece"[14] more than 200 years before the coming of Alexander's army. This use of African ideas came with the first Greek students of the Africans such as Thales, Pythagoras, and Isocrates. But not only were the names of the gods taken by the Greeks but the complex of ideas, concepts, and temperaments that went with the deities. Thus, even where the name of the god may have become Greek over time, e.g., *Djehuty* becoming *Thoth* becoming *Hermes*, the ethical and moral qualities of the deities became the foundation for Greek mythology. Despite the difficulty in finding lasting political union or *pax Graeco* because they fought violently among themselves, the ancient Greeks, with the guidance of the relocated African deities, gave to the West a developing sense of human fellowship and a respect for the intangible qualities of artistic life.

Two natural phenomena have dominated African civilizations from the beginning: water and the sun. Ancient Kemet was the principal example of the roles played by these two natural phenomena. In every compartment of its cosmology, medicine, religion, agriculture and society these two decisive factors straddled the civilization like giant crocodiles.

The first was the Nile itself. A thread that kept pieces of the various kingdoms finely knitted, it generated monumental responses to the environment. The annual flooding made possible, as nowhere else, the necessity of calculations and predictions. In its powerful role as life giver, the sun, like the river, came to represent well-being for the ancient Africans. I shall turn now to a more extensive discussion of each of the natural factors in their relationship to the society.

THE RIVER NILE, *HAPY*

The central physical phenomenon of Egypt was the great river, the Nile. It played a vital role in the creation of Kemetic philosophy, agriculture, technology, and religion. The Africans called their land Kemet and it was designated "the land of the Blacks." This was quite appropriate inasmuch as the country had found its life from the emergence of civilization in Upper, that is, southern Egypt, where the people were often as black as the fertile soil that extended, on either side, the length of the Nile.

Without the mighty river, Egypt in ancient time would have been nothing but desert, an extension of the Great Sahara, barren and relatively lifeless. With the Nile, 4,100 miles long over its entire course, Egypt became a remarkable civilization. The river rises at the equator among the great lake and river system close to the massive and majestic Congo River. The Uganda-Burundi Nile, as it can be called since it rises in Uganda and Burundi, meets the Ethiopian Nile, or Abay River, near Khartoum. At this point the river is nearly 1,300 miles from the Mediterranean Sea.

Ancient Nubia, Ta-Seti, which covers portions of present-day Sudan and southern Egypt, shepherds the Nile through tortuous topography. In fact, there are six areas where the river passes through rough sandstone and limestone formations called cataracts. The valley of the Nile is gradually extended from ten to thirty miles in width as it passes through southern Egypt. A hundred miles from the Mediterranean Sea the Nile forms the Delta area that constitutes lower or northern Egypt proper. The Nile divides into two main branches. The western mouth is called Rosetta; the eastern mouth where the river empties into the sea is called the Damietta that is also the name of the town conquered in 1219 by the European Crusaders.

The Nile overflows each year, beginning around June. The Ethiopian Nile, Abay, is the source of the overflow because it carries the increased volume of water caused by melted snow into the Nile. By September or October the Nile reaches its peak. The regularity of this inundation aided the development of precision and gave the priests enormous responsibility and power because they could predict when the river would overflow. Hapy, the generous god of the annual flood, was honored for bringing joy to all human beings.

Much like other Africans in riverine areas of the continent the Egyptians viewed the world with security, stability and optimism. The world did not seem harsh and ferocious, cruel and menacing, to the Egyptian. To a large extent the geography of Egypt provided the people with a pleasant isolation except to the south. There were no harbors in the Delta, deserts east and west, and so openness to the south through the cataracts allowed Ethiopians and Nubians to interact with the Egyptians. Irrigation, that is, the management of the water, provides a clue to the first grand project of a national or central character. Prior to and contemporaneous with the building of the pyramids was the emphasis on irrigation.

The Egyptians built large rectangular basinsto capture the over-flowing waters. Silt was deposited in the basinsand the Egyptians were able to use them for agricultural purposes.Egypt represents the longest continuous African civilization inthe ancient period. It lasted nearly four thousand years from about3400 B.C. to 333 B.C.

Manetho, Egyptian historian during the Greek Ptolomaic Period wrote abook, *The History of Egypt,* under the Commission of one of theGreek kings, Ptolemy Philadelphus. This book is lost. Manetho's list of the thirty dynasties of ancient Egypt does exist, however. We are able to estimate the date of Menes' unification of the Lower and Upper kingdoms constituting the first dynasty of Egyptian history from Manetho's list. Some estimates are as late as 3,200 B.C. for Menes' conquest of Lower Egypt to unite the country. Regardless to the disagreement over the origin of the dynasties most experts admit that civilization existed in Egypt long before Menes combined the two regions and wore the United Crown. Dynastic Egypt introduced a powerful monarchy that lasted for thousands of years until it was conquered by Assyrians, Persians, and then disintegrated with Alexander's Macedonian invasion of Africa.

The antiquity of Egypt creates problems of understanding because of the numerous breaks in the chain of dynasties, coups, foreign invasions and regional intrigues. Changes in religion, politics and art happened frequently enough to force Africanists and

Africologists to create their own periodizations. Large blocks of Egyptian history have been designated the Old Kingdom, Middle Kingdom, Empire, Ethiopian Period, Persian Period, and the Saitic Revival. I have renamed these periods: *United Kingdom, Middle Kingdom, Majestic Period, Grand Empire, Persian Period, Saitic Revival,* and *Ptolemaic Rule.* Despite the modifications suggested by these periods the constancy and continuity of Egypt are remarkable for a country. The Egyptians retained their essential African outlook in terms of myths, symbolisms, and ethos throughout the history of the country. Only with the arrival of the Greeks, and later in 639 AD, with the arrival of the Arabs in force did the mythopoeic pattern of Egypt undergo changes that have impacted the historiography of the region to this day.

The per-aa or *pharaoh* (in Hebrew) as deity always played a central role in Egypt's social and political life. The per-aa, the Great House, was key to the life of Egyptians. Things did not change that much. The River Nile was predictable; the seasons came and went as they had been ordered by the gods, and life was stable, static; the only dynamic being the individual's quest to follow the priest's instructions for preparation for the afterward. Any dramatic change was certain to cause consternation. For example, if the Nile failed to overflow on time this would be an occasion of great discussion and contemplation leading to sacrifices to the riverine deities. Ancient Egyptians were convinced that the single most important fact was the changelessness of the cosmos. Thus, they believed in and relied upon the fixed nature of all human society.

A student of this classical African civilization must always note the struggle between the traditional and the innovative and see how tradition, whether in medicine, religion, dance, agriculture, knowledge, or politics, gives little place to innovation. Ancient Egypt, like other classical African civilizations, placed a premium on the laws of the ancestors. Yet in its emphasis on tradition, Egypt perfected its pattern of governance and its reliance on static symbolisms.

THIS AND THE THINITE ERA

Centered at This, sometimes called Thinis, in southern Egypt, near the city of Abydos, were temples and priests who directed the formative phase of early dynastic Egypt. This was the Timbuctoo of early dynastic Egypt. It attracted the leading scholars, military generals, and builders in the first two dynasties. At This it is now believed that ciKam was developed as a sacred writing form. The first significant event the Africans recorded was the unification of Egypt by the mighty warrior-king, Menes, who is also called Narmer, Aha, or Scorpion. Menes, a king of the south, subdued the kingdom of the north, as he had done with several smaller kingdoms in the south, and unified the country, thus establishing the first nation in the world that combined numerous ethnic groups into one general government.

The "two lands" appears in Egyptian records to designate the historical, geographical, and cosmological significance of the act of uniting them. The Nile Valley had been, prior to Menes, and area with two broad double kingdoms, and before that, a land of numerous independent clans. Some Egyptians even referred to Egypt after Menes as a double monarchy with a single king. Each of the regions contained numerous *sepats,* called *nomes* by the Greek, that tended to be drawn according to lines represented by one ethnic group or another. These sepats had their own leaders, their own deities, and their own responses to the Nile. All of the s*epats* in the north reflected the crowns of that region while in the south the kings of *sepats* reflected the crown in that region.

The crown of southern Egypt was a white crown. The crown of northern Egypt was a red crown. The white crown was called *hedjet*; the red crown was called *deshert*. At this, the new double crown was introduced and named Sekhemti. It united the two crowns and persisted throughout Egyptian history as the official royal crown.

The double crown, *sekhemti*, represented a humanistic conquest where the conquering southerners allowed the crown of the northerners to flourish alongside theirs. Double offices were often maintained by the per-aa; two actual set of palaces; two celebrations of the Sed festival for the coronation of the king, with distinctive insignia and ritual in each area; and two ceremonies for the king's burial in southern and northern Egypt. One easily remembers the generous offer of Sekou Toure of Guinea making the deposed Kwame Nkrumah of Ghana a double president of Guinea. This action reminds one of the significance of a demonstration of magnanimous spirit to the sustaining of the African principle of community

Egyptian dualism was not based on history alone but cosmology. The Egyptians believed that equilibrium of opposites was fundamental to everything. While it is true that nature, particularly in terms of the Nile and the climate, showed itself as the principle of harmony, in a *ma'atic* sense, the idea of appositional dualities found expression first in the universe itself; thus it was more celestial than terrestrial. Some writers believe that the north-south axis, that is, lower-upper division of ancient Egypt was really seen in the light of a struggle between two gods, Seth of the north and Heru of the south. They place the history of the two lands in the context of strife. While strife often existed and frequently came out in the struggle for the *sekhemti,* it is incorrect to interpret any Kemetic text in the light of regional antagonism, especially in relation to the gods Heru and Seth. Such interpretation owes more to contemporary realities than to ancient ones.

THE MIGHTY SUN

The sun like the Nile was a dominant part of Kemetic life and thought. Its abundant heat and light produced in the people respect, awe, and inspiration. It influenced every aspect of Kemetic society. The fields did not give good crops without the sun, the wellbeing of the land was directly related to the sun, and so, the sun was also seen as a deity. It was at On, that is, Ionnu, also called Heliopolis that the sun priests had their central influence although throughout Kemet there was a major association with Ra.

Three forms of the sun god appeared in the two lands. Ra was represented in the early morning as Khepra, the scarab beetle. **Khepra** deposited its seed in tiny round pellets that were rolled with their back legs. The priests believed that the rising sun came forth like the scarab from its own substance and was reborn of it. To the Africans this was a perfect analogy for the movement of the sun across the sky. A second form of the sun god was as **Ra himself** with a human body and a falcon head. Crowned with a solar disc and a cobra, Ra gained preeminence by the Fifth Dynasty and was considered the head of the pantheon. Each morning, the Africans watched Ra slip from behind Manu, the Mountain of Sunrise, and sail across the sky, as it were, in his solar boat, accompanied by a divine retinue. As it was in other African societies such a powerful event had to be recorded as ritual drama that remains in dance, movement, and song, the heart of African spirituality. Written on the walls of the pyramids and tombs and papyri, these ritual events contained the totality of the human endeavor to express the divine. That is why finally, as Atum, the god was represented in human form wearing the red and white crowns of the two lands. The deity Ptah was often represented as a scarab beetle at the temple in Ionnu (Heliopolis).

Thus, in a mythopoeical manner at dawn the sun was a child represented by the scarab beetle Khepra; at midday it was an adult male represented by Ra; and at sunset it was Atum, an old man who disappeared into the horizon. The most mysterious part of all was the night voyage. By night Ra sailed through the underworld and made it just in time for the dawn trip across the sky. Nothing could be so certain, that is, so consistent to the African as the journey of deity Ra.

Creation itself was believed to be the work of the sun god. When Atum was present alone in the watery mass of Nun that filled the universe, he generated two other gods by spitting them out. Thus, Shu and Tefnut, representing air and moisture, respectively, came forth. By their union Shu and Tefnut produced two children, Geb, the earth god and Nut, the sky goddess. Geb and Nut had four children, Osiris and Isis and Seth and Nephthys. These nine deities constitute the Supreme Ennead who exercised control over the entire pantheon. Five of these deities are cosmological: Atum, Shu, Tefnut, Geb, and Nut. As the priests of ancient Kemet explained it, Geb (earth) and Nut (sky) were locked in a tight procreative embrace and Shu (air) came between them and pushed Nut skyward while Geb remained earthbound.

The other four deities were essentially involved in the relationship of the gods to human beings, especially through the office of the divine kingship. They were the major forces in society. Ausar represented the dead king and was always eternally resurrected in

Heru (Horus), the living son. Seth, the implacable foe of Ausar (Osiris), was the god of the deserts rather than the fertile lands. He was the Great Opponent who was abandoned by Nebhet, though his wife was able to assist Auset in sustaining Ausar. Atum does not figure as a major influence in this part of the order. His work is creation, not the maintenance of society. Although it is true that the per-aa, after Khafre (ca. 2,900 B.C.E.), was considered a "son of Ra" the *uraeus* of the cobra goddess, *Wadjyt*, that appears on the king's forehead represents one symbol of Ra and shows the sun god's significance in the kingship though this is not a direct responsibility. The Supreme Ennead is in fact a corporate entity with two distinct functions, maintenance and order, although Atum sets them both in motion.

INTERPRETING THE KEMETIC RECORD

Africologists can no longer study African societies as the carriers of detached, isolated, and quixotic culture separate from traditions. To do so is to commit a major intellectual crime inasmuch as the prototypes of the social/behavioral and cultural/ aesthetic ideas and ideals found in discrete African societies and communities are connected to classical Africa. The scholar must at least explore the possibility that her or his research pursuit finds its source in a classical tradition. There are two reasons for this procedure: (1) *re-confirmation* and (2) *delinking*. *Re-confirmation* means that the scholar pursues the organic, Diopian unity of African thought, symbols, and ritual concepts to their classical origins. *Delinking* implies that the study of African phenomena ceases being a subset of the European intellectual project that maintains the study of African people, continental or Diasporan, as marginal and peripheral.

An exploration, to be Africological, must be based on sound intellectual and philosophical foundations that maintain the centrality of the African experience and the primacy of the classical traditions. Whether the researcher is exploring African American child-rearing practices in North Philadelphia or African kinship patterns among the Galla in Ethiopia, *re-confirmation* and *delinking* are necessary steps in establishing the Afrocentric focus of the work. A researcher will find greater opportunity for re-confirmation or delinking in a given project but the process itself asserts the discipline in the research project and guards against easy slippage into Eurocentric thinking that could lead to misinterpretation of data. A study of language in Africa, for example, must begin with the possibility of Diopian unity, interconnected graphic designs and philosophical continuity. Such has been the work of Ama Mazama, Mubabinge Bilolo, Theophile Obenga, and Cheikh Anta Diop. Mazama is a Sorbonne trained linguist and a leading Afrocentric theorist who has established the Congo origin of much of the language of the people of Guadeloupe. On the other hand, Bilolo's influence on the study of Middle Egyptian is without peer on the African continent with his argument for the direct relationship of ancient ciKam, the language of Kemet, to the chiLuba language of Congo. Obenga is connected to the pioneering work of Cheikh Anta Diop and the combination of Obenga from the Congo Brazzaville and Diop from Senegal brings two of the most important African linguist together in the study of African correspondences of languages. Diop, however, is the foundational scholar for Africans interested in the possibility of African unity. Although these scholars have different emphases in their researches they all have utilized Afrocentric concepts, some without understanding the nature of their use for practical developments in African action. For example, the late Jacob Carruthers rightly claimed the primacy of the ancient Egyptian language as the beginning point for any real discussion about African studies but was unable to see the larger paradigmatic Afrocentric view proposed by Karenga, Mazama, and Bilolo. Yet in the wake of the proposals of these scholars a whole new line of thinking has developed in the Afrocentric School of Thought; a line of thinking that was inherent, though not fully realized until now, in any fundamental examination of the nature of scholarship about African people. Egypt was indeed the light of Africa and Africa the light of Egypt, as Cheikh Anta Diop had maintained.[15] More so, Kemet was not to be something merely observed but a venue for an African renaissance. The time has come for African intellectuals to go beyond the think-tank posture to the do-tank position that will make our work transformative.

Most Afrocentric scholars have maintained that without connecting all African studies to classical African civilizations, languages, and cultures our research remains essentially tangential and peripheral and as a consequence unable to inspire the rebirth and re-emergence of Africa. As a Diopian I have found the arguments of these writers convincing and compelling. Therefore, I have attempted to advance the line of thinking, based upon my own studies of the ancient language of Egypt, ciKam, by examining the various transformations of the classical language in other African languages and indeed in the languages of Europe as well. You will note that I call this language after Mubabinge Bilolo "ciKam" or as I prefer "mdwKam" because the language should not be called by a simple description as in "divine words." It is indeed the language of Kemet. This approach, however, becomes necessary in light of the many distortions of African culture and history that appear in the writings of some European scholars who began their work in the womb of a racist ideology. Their entire point of view toward Africa was negative and few of the early Egyptologists could divorce their hegemonic attitudes towards knowledge about other people from their political position in the world.

It is the political positions and racist attitudes of many European and white American scholars that have created the tremendous misunderstanding regarding the African presence in world history. Almost all of the Eurocentric writers, e.g., Breasted, Lichtheim, Budge, Piankoff, and DeBuck, among others, saw Egypt as a part of some mysterious "oriental" culture entirely unrelated to the continent where it was situated. Consequently, writers like them went so far as to devise complex explanations for the separation of Egypt from the rest of Africa. The Nile River was seen as a barrier because of the cataracts; the desert was called a natural barrier to Egypt's contact with its neighbors to the South and West; and the relationship of Egypt to Syria looms larger than its relationship to Ethiopia in the minds of these Eurocentric writers.

The late scholar Jacob Carruthers brilliantly identifies three fundamental faults in the thinking of the Eurocentric Egyptologists: (1) they confused "Nhsi" and "ha," (2) they failed to understand the subtleties of the ancient language and employed European concepts to African behaviors, and (3) they failed to understand the "dramatic meanings beneath the formal and obvious meanings" in the ancient texts.[16] In any interpretation of the connection between African social and cultural systems the lack of a basic perspective *centered on Africa itself* is problematic. For example, as Carruthers points out, the eminent African thinkers Chancellor Williams and DeGraft-Johnson made incorrect analyses based upon their reliance of the mistranslations of the Kemetic texts by white Egyptologists. These scholars accepted the translation of "nhsi" as "Negro" a racial distinction, rather than see that the ancient Africans of Egypt would never make such a distinction between themselves and the Africans who lived to the South and West of them. The Eurocentric Egyptologists only in-

terpreted "nhsi" as "Negro" out of their own perspective toward
reality. They lived and wrote during a time when racial distinctions were very much a part of the social landscape. Even today
some white Egyptologists try to distinguish between Egyptian
and other Africans as if to say Egypt is not in Africa. But "nhsi"
represents the varied features of the Egyptians as well as other Africans. All one has to do is to look at the murals, the engravings,
and statuettes which provide abundant physical evidence of the
antiquity of Egypt's Africanity. The people of ancient Egypt were
no different than the African people of the United States, Brazil,
Mali, Nigeria, Ethiopia, Sudan, or Zimbabwe. Carruthers contends that "the linguistic data settle the argument, *Nhsi* Nehesi) is
not a race or color distinction but a national distinction since the
word for Black in the context of color is "Km" which is the root of
the word which the Egyptians called themselves."[17]

Maulana Karenga has adequately dealt with the problem of the
subtleties of the language in his retranslation *The Husia,* a book
that represents the best example to date of a systematic attempt
to infuse the translations of the ancient texts with African as opposed to European concepts. Karenga is profoundly historical in
his approach to the texts and although this has engendered a certain amount of criticism, he is correct to assume, as he does, that
any antihistorical hostility is due to an incomplete understanding
of the process of Afrocentric reconstruction. Our analysis, therefore, of the connections between the ancient Egyptian language

and other African languages must be organic and historical.

This brings us to the problem of the Rosetta Stone mythology itself. Given to the world as the key to ancient Egypt, the Rosetta Stone myth starts with Napoleon's Army in 1799. Actually, the build up for the Rosetta Stone myth starts with 1638 when John Greaves drew up the measurements of the Great Giza Pyramid. In the eighteenth century Richard Pococke studied the Dahshur and Sakkara sites, attempting to make scientific measurements of the various groups of monumental works. But it was Napoleon's Army, like the army of Alexander of Macedonia nearly 2,000 years earlier, that shocked the world of ancient Egyptian studies. While Alexander's army had raided the libraries and museum and taken the books to Athens, Napoleon's army, probably remembering the great bounty taken by armies before, had several authors and would-be-scholars among the soldiers.

Dominique-Vivant Denon accompanied Napoleon's General Desaix on his campaign into Upper Egypt and was totally overwhelmed by the monuments of this classic African civilization. Dominique-Vivant Denon saw it as the most fabulous sight human eyes had even seen. Nothing in Greece or Rome compared to what the savant saw in Upper Egypt. In 1803 he published his book *Description de l'Egypt*. The Jomard group of publishers immediately found it successful and the work became a standard as it opened up a new field of study. Dominique-Vivant Denon illustrated his work with meticulous drawings and the European world that had basked in the glories of Greece and Rome realized that there was a far older and grander civilization of which they knew little. Since the script and the language of Egypt was African, and in their minds "exotic," Europeans felt intense competition to decipher the script. It was like an enormous criminal case in which the police detectives had to deliver a suspect, had to break open the case, had to show that the case was not beyond their powers of deciphering. It is easy to understand this social and racial pressure on the scholars and writers of Europe.

Thus, during the same campaign in which Dominique-Vivant Denon had found his inspiration, one of the engineers of Napoleon's army is said to have found the Rosetta Stone. This stone became the possession of the British Museum after France's withdrawal from Egypt. But the British did not move it to London before casts had been made and Champollion was able to decipher the script. Upon Champollion's "break-through" in 1822 the European world went wild with excitement. Then in 1828-29 Champollion led an expedition to Egypt for eighteen months in order to copy inscriptions. The Germans soon followed the British and French with scholars and plunderers. In fact, the twelve-volume work on Egyptian monuments that was the basis of the great Berlin collection was paid for by the Prussian government. Auguste Mariette was sent by the Louvre to collect Egyptian antiquities and soon received authority to establish the Egyptian Museum and Antiquities Service, becoming its first director. This gave the Europeans direct access to the entire field of African classical artifacts and would make the task of overturning erroneous interpretations, based on ethnocentric interests, doubly difficult. William Matthew Flinders Petrie was the first person to hold a chair of Egyptology in England at the University College, London. This chair of Egyptology had been founded and funded by the wealthy Amelia Edwards, who wanted very much to be the major player in this part of African research. She set up the Egypt Exploration Fund and this was later followed by the *Deutsche Orient Gesellschaft* and the *Mission Archeologique Francaise* which became the Institut Francais d'Archeologie Orientale.

Already in the late 1880s the European scholars had decided to place Egypt in the Orient, that is, Egyptian Studies was to become a branch of Oriental Studies, not African Studies. The European creation of Oriental Studies and the inability to see Africa in the light of its ancient past meant that the degradation of the African was nearly complete. Few European scholars could see Kemetic civilization as African in the nineteenth century. Although "oriental" has come to mean to the Europeans "Islamic" as well as Japan, India, and China, there was no such confusion in African antiquity. The Nile Valley civilizations predate Arab conquest and represent the indigenous developments of the Africans. The Berlin Conference of 1884-85 underscored the condition of all of Africa as the European powers divided up the continent among themselves without a thought to the democratic rights of the peoples in the various territories. All of the plundering and raiding of ancient monuments and sites in Africa could happen because of two important facts.

The first is the complete abandonment of the classical African civilizations by the conquering Arabs from the seventh century to the eighteenth century. With limited exceptions the Arabs were able to control the whole of North Africa from the first *jihads* out of Arabia between 641 and 900 CE. They appeared to have little respect or appreciation for the classical civilization they found in the Nile Valley. Having destroyed the organic structure of the African society they found in Egypt and Nubia, reinstituted the ban on the Egyptian language, and allowed the great ancestral holy places to lie in ruin, the Arabs created the perfect opportunity for the distortion of the African heritage of the Nile Valley civilizations by the Europeans who came after them. As the second reason for this state of affairs in Egyptian studies, the subsequent suppression of the Arabs by the Ottoman Turks, Mameluks, and Europeans made it possible for the colonizers to dictate the terms of the study of ancient Egypt, even to assume the leadership of the antiquities services.

As African people were colonized and enslaved both on the continent and in the Americas, there were few voices raised against the appropriation of African history as there were few voices raised against the appropriation of our land and labor. Just as we had to throw off the yoke of oppression from our bodies and our lands Africans will have to liberate the study of the classical civilizations because the European colonization of geography, that is, land, went hand-in-hand with the colonization of information and knowledge. Visit any museum in any major European city and there you will see the great treasures of Africa, taken over a five-hundred-year period. Read any book on African people and you will see the robbing of African civilization, history, and culture. This is why it seems in most European works that African peoples had no culture, no history, no dynamism prior to European domination and exploitation. A people's classical history is important for the reason that it forms a part of the grand continuity of concepts, values, experiences, visions, and possibilities. Having separated Egypt from Africa in their minds, the Eurocentric Egyptologists began the process of making African societies, other than Egypt, static entities that never changed over time. This was in some ways an intellectually criminal act because it violated the best traditions of evidence and beyond that it violently detached a part of the continent from the rest of the continent.

Ibn Khaldun and the Racist Pitch against Africans

The Europeans were certainly not alone in this process. The history of Ibn Khaldun is a significant example of the historiography of the conqueror. Although the Khaldunic history provides some interesting viewpoints from the fourteenth century about Africa it is nonetheless a historiography of conquest of the African peoples. The Nubians, Berbers, Tamasheks, Shilluks, Dinkas, and Nuers who fought to keep their territories in the face of the onslaught of Islamic armies do not even receive footnotes in the Khaldunic version of history. In fact, it is these people "without history" who have played major roles in, the transforming phenomena of the African continent. Their histories, once told, will fill in the cultural and linguistic gaps as well as the linkages between the various African nations and kingdoms. As late as the 1890s Azande kings were refusing to wear Arab clothes, preferring to wear the leopardskin as an insignium of royalty. An important Azande king like Mdarama found the Arab clothing imposed upon his culture to be a violation of his traditions well into the 1890s. Of course, as in other matters, the conquerors soon had their way and the Azande adopted both Arab and European styles before the twentieth century was in full swing. Even so, it is the history of people like the Azande, the Nubians, the Dinka, the Beja, the Uduk, the Shilluk, and the Sara who will provide us the behavioral and linguistic keys to the ancient Nile Valley's connection to the rest of Africa.

PRESENTING AND INTERPRETING THE PRIMARY DATA

In such an exploration of cultural factors it is necessary to make some primary interpretations. Because of our Diopian orientation we are certain to make different interpretations from those imposed by European tradition. For example, the Nuer people refer to Kwoth as the principal deity in their culture. Kwoth is the guide of the human race; Kwoth manages the affairs of the Nuer through attention to the rules of nature; and Kwoth is the measurer of a person's life. In every respect Kwoth is like Thoth, Djehuti, the Kemetic deity who became known as the father of writing and as highly civilized life they found there, and then became civilized in turn. It is possible to forgive Hyma for some of his sins because much of what we know about the ancient world now was not known when he first began to write. We now know, for example, that the first cities in history were not developed in Mesopotamia by the Sumerians around 4500 B.C. but rather in the region of the Nubian desert in northern Sudan and Southeastern Egypt around 20,000 B.C. Data first recorded by the United States Columbia shuttle in 1978 point to buried cities under the desert. These settlements represent the first known communities where human beings organized societies according to skills and specialties. Scientists believe that these settlements predate any that have been discovered so far. What is unforgivable in Hyma's conceptualization of ancient history is the idea that Egypt is in the Orient. Clearly this is the bias of categorization created initially in the nineteenth century and maintained in the present century by institutions such as the School for Oriental and African Studies in London and the various other "Oriental" institutes set up in Europe and the United States. So while Hyma could admit, as he did, that Europe received from Egypt "its earliest knowledge of civilized life" he could not admit that Egypt was "African." In fact, in a telling paragraph, Hyma concludes of the paintings of Egyptians "Their skin had been white, but powerful rays of the sun quickly turned the color to tan." Whatever is meant by this statement it seems clear that Hyma denies the blackness of the ancient Egyptians, a fact that has been established scientifically by the leading Egyptologists of the contemporary era.

The heresy found in the works of European writers of the 18th, 19th, and 20th centuries was never in the mind of the Greeks, the earliest classical writers of Europe. Indeed, the Greeks saw Egypt, an African country, as the cradle of wisdom and knowledge. The most famous of the Hellenes crossed the sea to be initiated, if they could, at the temples of Egypt. Such was the attraction of this center of information and culture for the Greeks, Sicilians, Cyprians, and Persians. Even the most quintessential Greek figures, such as Orpheus and Homer, are said to have travelled to Egypt. Both Solon and Plato crossed the Mediterranean to pay their homage to ancient Egypt. Thales, Pythagoras, Oenopidus, and Eudoxus are only a few of the early Greek thinkers who found it necessary to study in Africa. Indeed, according to Diogenes Laerce in *Thales* we find that Thales learned his astronomy and geometry from the Egyptian priests. We also know from the Greeks that Pythagoras spent twenty-two years in the temples of Egypt. Olympiodorus in his *Life of Plato* and Strabo in his description of Egypt say that Plato spent thirteen years in Egypt learning geometry and theology. The celebrated writers of Greece became more popular at home when they could proclaim to their communities that they had been educated by African priests. One could return to Ephesus, Thyatira, Antioch, Miletus, Hierapolis, and Halicarnassus with status once he had visited Waset, Sais, Mennefer, and other centers of Kemet.

There is no great emphasis in the period prior to the 18th century for taking Egypt and Nubia out of Africa and making those ancient civilizations "oriental" if they could not be European. Therefore, it is obvious that the predicament of Africa, the great European commerce in human slavery, and the need to minimize the contribution of Africans in order to justify the institution of slavery meant that the European writers would deliberately falsify historical records. In many ways they participated in a vulgar scholarship culminating in the works of the famous servant of Eurocentric scholarship on Africa, Sir E. A. Wallis Budge. He became the chief "Egyptologist" of the British Museum at a time when "orientalism" was at its highest level. Budge brought the work of Barthelemy to fruition in his many projects. As Keeper of the Egyptian and Syrian Antiquities in the British Museum, Budge made his career on interpretations, translations. Karenga refers to Budge's works as "mistranslations." However, the fact that Budge presented many reproductions of the Egyptian art helped to popularize African cultural forms.

Many books on Egypt bear his name. Budge became famous for his work on *Dwellers on the Nile, Egyptian Magic, The Gods of the*

Egyptians, Osiris and the Egyptian Resurrection, and *The Egyptian Book of the Dead.* Thus the scholar who wants to explore the possibilities of African connections, African philosophy, or African culture must first venture through the maze created by Budge and others such as James Breasted of the University of Chicago. Yet the later scholars such as Antonio Loprieno and Maulana Karenga have given us more useful understandings of the language and culture of ancient Egyptians.

Budge's assessment of the importance of the Rosetta Stone, once a source of mystery and intrigue among many Egyptian scholars, is an astounding exposure of the European attitude toward African language. The Rosetta Stone, now in the British Museum's Egyptian Gallery, was the source of enormous controversy when it was first brought to Europe. During the French campaign in Egypt, a French artillery officer found the Rosetta Stone in the ruins of Fort St. Julien, near the Rosetta mouth of the Nile. To understand the full significance of this rather ordinary-looking four-foot-long stone it is important to grasp the known facts of its generation. The stone was apparently made to record the activities of Ptolemy V. Epiphanes, a representative of the Greek, Alexander of Macedonia. This particular Ptolemy ruled the land from 205 to 182 B.C.E.

The stone contains information on the many projects carried out by Ptolemy V. Epiphanes, the gratitude expressed to him by the priests who ordered that statues of the king be placed in the temples of Egypt, and that copies of the decree be made on basalt stelae and set up in temples near the king's statues. The Rosetta Stone is taken to be one of the stelae that was supposed to be made in honor of the decree. Questions could be raised regarding the historical veracity of the account that appears on the stone. So far only one of these several stones has been recovered despite the fact that they were to be set up in three temples.

Budge is quick to point out that the real value in the stone lies in its philological importance because it opens the door to understanding ancient Egyptian. This was the key to deciphering the great body of African literature that had come down through the centuries. In fact, Budge says in his typically Eurocentric manner, "until the beginning of the last century there was neither an Oriental nor a European who could either read or understand a hieroglyphic inscription." It is absolutely awesome to think that the Europeans never thought of examining African languages and graphics, since they were examining Egyptian, for connections to the ancient language. ciKam is related to many other African languages both in its structure and in its ideographs. The only reason one can give for this blatant disregard for the languages of the people on the continent itself is the pervasive attitude that Africans did not create ancient Egypt. The Europeans of the Aryan school, as Martin Bernal has called them, were willing to look to the Syrians, the Phoenicians, the Indians, and the Arabs before they turned their eyes to the neighbors of Egypt in Africa for linguistic or cultural relatedness. Furthermore, the arrogance of the statement that "neither an Oriental nor a European" borders on being dumb when speaking of a classical African civilization.

Meanwhile, white writers, prior to the European recovery of the Rosetta Stone, wrote preposterous interpretations of the ancient language. Some said that every word was a biblical expression, others claimed that Hebrew compositions were found on the temple walls, and still others said that the hieroglyphics were alphabetic characters but it is not until Champollion, a student of Coptic and an avid believer in the value of parallel linguistic, published a piece on the meaning of a red granite obelisk found by J. W. Bankes in 1815 and set up in Dorsetshire, England, that some real progress was made. This is not to say that others had not been on the road to deciphering the ancient language. Certainly the work of Akerblad, Zoega, and Young are names that must be mentioned in conjunction with the project. However, it is Champollion who saw that the obelisk had Greek and Egyptian inscriptions and that one of the names was Ptolemy. He was able to read Ptolemy in both Greek and hieroglyphics and this made him believe that he could interpret the Rosetta Stone if he could discover the exact meaning of the Greek. So when he had examined the *tekenu* (obelisk) and found one of the names on it that he had seen on the Rosetta Stone he was certain that he had the key. Thus, by 1822 he had discovered the name of Cleopatra in one of the *shenus* on the Rosetta Stone and the door to the interpretation was unlocked. The fact that the first translations were done by non-Afrocentrists underscores why Africologists should study the language. Carruthers believed that the mastery of the ancient language should be a major enterprise for African scholars. He states "we should use that language as our classical language just as the Europeans use Greek and Latin today." Obenga has placed the issue of ancient Egyptian as the classical language of Africa at the front door of linguistic research in Africa: *"Cette question est la veritable question de la recherche linguistique aujourd'hui en Afrique."* It must also be placed on the front burner of our own work because it is impossible to reestablish historical and cultural linkages without first understanding the relationship of present behavior to the classical concepts. All language defines the users.

When the Europeans first entered the arena of modern Egyptian studies Africans were little equipped to make our own researches. Fortunately, the new impetus in Egyptian studies comes from African scholars convinced that the secret to all African culture is through the door of Kemet. In fact, the Africologist brings to such study the community or circle of memory, openness to a wide range of African scholarship, not centered on a small isolated village or group, but rather broad and multidisciplinary perspectives from an Afrocentric angle, and a commitment to excellence. Scholars of the Association for the Study of Classical African Civilizations are rich in linguistics, historical, anthropological, sociological, political theory and cultural analysis backgrounds; some of the writers have special capabilities in philosophy and ethics. This means that the advances to be made in classical civilizations will be made by many of these writers and scholars. Their work in Africa itself, their mastery of the languages of the continent, and their commitment to the African Cultural Project will ensure understanding the generative power of the Kemetic chronology.

KEMETIC CHRONOLOGICAL TABLE

(*Foundation of the Empire*)

UNITED KINGDOM and the First Golden Period

First Golden Age started when Menes (Narmer) conquered 42 sepats along the Nile River around 3200 BCE

The First Golden Period Spanned Five Dynasties, 1 to 5

(Third Dynasty 2686-2613 BCE)

Sanakhte

Zoser

Sekhemkhet Huni

(Fourth Dynasty 2613-2494 B.C.)

Sneferu Cheops Chephren Micerinus

(Fifth Dynasty 2494-2345 B.C.)

Userkafi Sahure

Nyuserre Unas

First Period of Instability

This was the time of the first period of political instability that lasted from 2181 to about 2133 B.C. The period included the 7th to 10th Dynasties.

MIDDLE KINGDOM and the Second Golden Period

(Eleventh Dynasty 2133-1991 B.C.)

Mentuhotep I

Inyotef

Mentuhotep II

(Twelfth Dynasty 1991-1786 B.C.)

Amenemet I

Senursert I

Senursert III

Amenemhet

(Thirteenth Dynasty 1786-1633 B.C.)

Sebekhotep III

Neferhotep

Second Period of Instability

A second period of political unrest existed when Kemet was governed in part by the Asiatic Hyksos occurred in this time. The

14th, 15th, 16th, and 17th dynasties consisted of intermittent rule by Hyksos and indigenous rulers.

MAJESTIC PERIOD and the Third Golden Period

New Kingdom

Third Golden Period

(Eighteenth Dynasty 1567-1320 B.C.)

Amoses

Amenhotep

Thuthmoses I

Thuthmoses II

Hatshepsut

Thuthmoses III

Amenhotep II

Thuthmosis IV

Amenhotep III

Akhenaton

Smenkhkare

Tutankhamen

Ay

Horemhab

GRAND EMPIRE and the Fourth Golden Period

Fourth Golden Period

(Twenty-Fifth Dynasty 790 BC to 526 BCE)

Piankhy

Tarharka

Shabaka

Shabataka

DECLINE OF KEMET

Asarhaddon, the king of the Assyrians, invaded Egypt and met the armies of Tarharka in 673 BC. Later Cambyses II of Persia fought the Egyptians at the Battle of Pelusium and the Persians conquered Egypt in 525 BCE. These successive attacks on the ancient culture of Kemet weakened the civilization and it was ripe for the plucking by other kingdoms. After this period came the invasion of the Macedonians in 333 BC and the Ptolemaic Dynasty, named after Alexander's general, Ptolemy. The Romans took Kemet from the Greeks in 30 BC with the defeat of Cleopatra and Antony and made Egypt a part of the Roman Empire.

THE WRITING QUESTION

Kemet provides us with the richest sources of ancient African ideals and concepts, thereby giving the Africologist entirely new bases for developing theory. However, the question of civilization is always raised in conjunction with the question of writing. While Kemet gives us the clear example of ciKam as a language form, we are often confused as to the meaning of this for other parts of Africa.

Two problems have existed in previous interpretations of African graphic systems: (1) The conscious attempt to isolate Egypt,

Ethiopia and Meroe (Nubia) from the rest of Africa, and (2) the promulgation of the view that Africans never invented writing systems. Both of these problems find their source in the condescending attitudes of Eurocentric authors whose purposes, economic or religious, found no place for a genuine analysis of the writing systems of Africa. Most of the early European authors were missionaries seeking to understand "primitive" languages in order to bring us into the more perfect light of European religion.

The rise of human civilization in the Nile Valley of northeast Africa is pretty much agreed upon by reputable scholars. Today, no one questions the anteriority of the African civilization of that region. Since human civilization carries with it certain necessary relational skills and functions, it is reasonable to assume that these early Nile Valley civilizations possessed some form of writing, some method of transmitting ideas. It would be impossible to expand culture without some communication system. While the oral communication system predates the visual system, the impact of Egypt, Axum, and Nubia, as recipient cultures of the earlier visual forms, found expression on the walls and in the furniture and domestic artifacts of cultures in other parts of Africa.

The word script refers to a system of visual symbols used to communicate, record, and entertain. A script conforms to an established convention if it is to be meaningful and functional and script is comprised of units called "mdus," that is, the smallest single units of the script system. Other authors choose to use different labels for the smallest single unit of script. I have merely employed the logical system of using concepts from the most ancient classical African language available.

Three major distinguishable writing systems exist in Africa: (1) pictograms, (2) ideograms, and (3) syllabic scripts. The pictogram is written (drawn, painted, shaped) on human skin, walls, mud, sand, metal, bark or paper, in a manner representative of some object of the visual world. It is therefore not considered abstract. Throughout Africa one can find, as I have found, great variation in pictograms. These pictograms often form sequential stories, or warnings, or greetings. The area of central Africa, encompassing Congo, Gabon, Cameroons, and the Central African Republic are particularly rich in pictogrammatic expressions. The *bwiti* religious symbolism in Gabon, the painted house walls of western Cameroons, or the specially carved naturalistic picture sequences often used in Malawi by the *sing'anga,* doctor, to greet his clients constitute narrative examples of the pictogram. Examples of this form can be found in almost all African societies.

The ideogram is written (drawn, shaped, painted, carved) on various materials and is used to state an idea. Thus, the perceptible word is represented in this manner. Among the Akan several ideograms are often used to state highly complex ideas. This, of course, is an extensive graphic form in Africa. Some authors claim the difference between ideographs and pictograms reside in the fact that the pictogram is more literal, showing less abstraction. Therefore the pictographs relationship to an object is direct, easily transmitted by virtue of its literalness. On the other hand the ideogram, where it is related to a concrete object, is usually symbolic, that is, the object represents something other than itself. So culturally based are most ideograms that an individual would normally have to be instructed in the meaning of the ideograms in order to read. For example, the Chinese ideogram for "happy" combines elements that show a mother and son, since this is the happiest relationship in Chinese traditional culture.

In the ancient Egyptian language, ideograms came to represent profound philosophical concepts. Thus, Anubis was shown with the face of a dog and came to be known as the one who accompanies the dead to the next world. Heru, son of Auset and Ausar, was written as a falcon-headed god, while Thoth (Djehuti), the father of writing, appeared as an ibis with a writing palette in his hand. Without an appreciation for *ciKam,* the ancient Egyptian language, it will be difficult to understand the ideograms.

IDEOGRAPHS

Nsibidi is an ideographic script that has come under close scrutiny in recent years because of its wide provenance as a graphic system. It is a graphic system used by various philosophical societies in east-central Nigeria to communicate philosophy. But it is not as Kubik says "a secret graphic system."[18] At one time nsibidi flourished among the Ibo and Edo as well as the Efik people, who are now the keepers of the script. Its considerable antiquity, confirmed by several scholars, suggests that its philosophical content may have come from the convergence of several systems. In fact, the thesis, expounded by several scholars that ancient Egyptian priests and their traditions returned to the central region of Africa with the coming of the Arab jihads is significant in this regard. It means that nsibidi is connected to the origin of the African philosophic system since similar writing appears throughout Africa. We know now that every region of the continent had some form of script long before the missionaries, slave traders and settlers came to pillage and distort. In Angola and Zambia, an ideographic system called *sona* is practiced by several ethnic groups, including the Cokwe, Lucazi, Mbwela, and Mbunda.[19] In the Cokwe language the system is called *sona*; in the other languages it is *tusona*. Unlike *nsibidi,* a system for philosophical knowledge, *tusona* also transmits empirical mathematics. The important work of Kubik and Jaritz attest to the prominence of this system in south central Africa. Numerous people use ideographic writing in the sand as means of warning, information, and leisure mathematic play. Hunters, returning to their village, often stop to make ideographic mathematic puzzles in the sand of a dry river-bed.

The Akan people of Ghana and the Ivory Coast have a tradition of *djayobwe*, bronze figures used for weighing gold, that are graphic, either in a pictograph or an ideograph form. The *dja* are indigenous to Ghana, Ivory Coast and Togo. Niangoran-Bouah says all the elements of the *dja*, both figurative and geometrical, are weights.[20] These forms, while local in their provenance, have philosophical connections and conceptual relationship to other symbolic forms in Africa. It is clear from historical records that the Akan came from the Sahara region. Insofar as black autochthonous groups are found in Morocco, Libya, Chad, Niger, Algeria and Tunisia, we can speculate that the interlinking of conceptual ideas have existed for millennia throughout West Africa. Indeed, correspondences have been shown between the languages and cultures of Akan and Yoruba with ancient Kemetic traditions. The masked figures in the cave paintings of the Sahara Desert show that the region belonged to black people in the Neolithic Period before it became desert and as Niangoran-Bouah says "The Sahara belongs to Black Africa."[21] So the value of the *djayobwe* in a discussion of the graphic systems of Africa is the linkage to the ancient classical civilization of Egypt. One will never be able to appreciate the intricate value of the *dja* without an adequate appreciation of the *ciKam*.

Phonological Scripts

The most prominent phonological scripts, those that represent the sounds of a language, are Vai, Toma, Mende and Bamun in Liberia, Guinea, Sierra Leone and Cameroons. When Europeans first examined African writing systems they looked for the phonological systems because these held greater similarity to their own systems.

Phonological systems are either alphabetical like English or syllabic like Japanese. In any case the script corresponds to a certain sound. Examining Africa from a Eurocentric viewpoint they concluded that there were no written languages in Africa until the nineteenth century. All serious researchers have now abandoned that preposterous thesis. It was an extravagant thesis, at any rate, because the ancient Meroitic text, the Ge'ez of Ethiopia, and the ancient Egyptian systems of writing predated any European system.

There is a political dimension to script preference that resides in the nature of the script. Since phonological scripts are language dependent they tend to maximize standardization and expansion. On the other hand, pictographs and ideographs are language independent and although they may be understood, like Chinese, by many people, they are not necessarily efficient. The great number of characters means that any form of duplication becomes problematic whereas in English the idea is to eliminate smaller dialects and have a one-to-one correlation between a unit of script and pronunciation.

The question of which script is the most "civilized" has also occupied the European mind. One can easily see that such a discourse is not an African issue, neither has it been expressed in Asian cultures; this is profoundly a European interest in hierarchy. Once those who subscribe to Martin Bernal's Aryan School of Thought accepted the fact that Africans have graphic writing, then the question became, "Is it the highest form?" This reminds

me of the comment that the late professor, dean, and superintendent of Washington's public schools, Barbara Sizemore, used to
make about black children reading. "It is not so much that they
read, according to whites, but how fast they read." We recognize,
however, that all graphic systems can be explained according to
the principle of functionality, one of the key planks in Ama Mazama's understanding of the Afrocentric paradigm.[22]

EXAMPLE OF SCRIPTS

Written scripts, whether as pictograms, ideograms, or phonological scripts are not the only means of sending a message. The
"object script" is also widely used in Africa, and has been, at least,
since pre-dynastic Egypt. The object script is when a communica-
tor uses a certain object in a particular way to send messages. For
example, the placing of stones in a special arrangement, the break-
ing of sticks, or the twisting of fabric can all be used to convey
messages. This form of communication crossed the West African
Sea (the Atlantic Ocean) to find a home in the Americas. Enslaved
Africans often found escape routes by "reading" the object scripts
of twisted branches or pieces of cloth left by others. On the continent itself, especially in West Africa, children have used object
scripts to mark access to their secret places for centuries.

There are several African object scripts that serve as mnemonic
systems. Among the Yoruba we find the *aroko*, a highly complex
way of sending a message used by military leaders, kings, and

princes. It is usually a string of cowrie shells twisted with feathers into various configurations, but there are variations. Theophile
Obenga found that *aroko* could be a simple symbolic message or
an elaborately structured system of cowrie shells. He also found
that each arrangement of cowries and feathers represented one
word.[23] Thus it was possible that in reading a message one had to
articulate the number of cowries like syllables. Kubik says *ara* is a
powerful system, that is mnemonic, but at the same time phonetic, and a form of script without paper. *Ara* is not the only practical
system of object scripts. *Mekutu alele* of Cameroons, *ngombo* of
Angola are two of the major object scripts using carved objects
placed in highly sacred divining bowls.[24]

Kubik has raised an important issue regarding these object
scripts. He is correct to see that the issue as to whether or not
these object scripts can be called graphic or script resides in the
nature of the European question. In European languages script
has a strong Latin background *(escrito*, Portuguese; *ecriture*,
French; and even in *shrift*, German) and particular referenta. Yet
the concept in African languages has its own specific terminology and categories. Consequently a cultural analyst should not
force African fields into European definitions. I do not accept a
narrow definition for script. There is no reason to impose a European particularism on African language behavior. Africans were
the first human beings to "script" as a matter of communicative
record. The ancient Egyptians left the most extensive and impres-

sive records of antiquity. We know almost all that we know of dynastic Egypt because of the ideograms and pictograms which first appeared around 6,000 B.C. Almost as early as the Egyptians were the Sumerians whose cuneiform syllabic script system written in soft clay, gives us another ancient view, but neither the Egyptian nor the Iraqi (Sumer) examples can be traced to Europe. The Egyptian hieroglyphic system, however, lasted much longer than the Iraqi (Sumer) and can be traced in various scripts of Africa. The alphabetic script, as opposed to the ideogram and pictogram scripts, emerged around 2,000 B.C. in Asia and spread to Europe.

The Eurocentric evolutionist theories postulated High and Primitive cultures. In such a formulation all African civilizations, with the possible exceptions of Egypt and Axum, were considered "primitive" cultures. These designations were often made on the basis of either the lack of permanent architecture or the lack of a writing system. But since definitions tend to be based on the cultural position and perspective of the person doing the defining, the European scholar often looked at Europe, what he knew, and tried to use it as a standard for evaluating other cultures. Thus, African societies, when they were no longer considered "primitive" were termed "simple" as opposed to "complex." Europeans societies were considered "advanced" and more "complex" than African societies, a sort of evolution in explanatory theories.

The implications of this view are numerous. In the first place it means that pictographs are considered the simplest forms of writing. Ideographs are more complex and finally the ultimate stage is the phonological script that leads directly to alphabetical scripts.

Although several writers have examined in some detail the emergence and development of writing in Africa, there remains, largely because of the surrogate racist categorization of Levy-Bruhl and Malinowski, among others, skepticism about African graphic systems. Clearly, however, the anteriority of Egypt is established in this field as it is in every field of human science and art. Diop recognizes the primacy of Egypt in this fashion:

> L'Egypte est au reste de l'Afrique Noire ce que la Grece et Rome sont a l'Occident. Les nouvelles humanites Africaines devront s'edifier sur les soubassements de l'antique culture pharaonique. L'egyptien ancien et le meroitique devront remplacer le latin et le grec dans les programmes. Le droit egyptien devra prendre la place du droit romain.[25]

This profound statement places all African language systems with their various graphic systems in line for a full philosophical and linguistic relationship with the African classical cultures. Furthermore, all thinking about philosophy, law, science, and the humanities must be centered in the agency of the ancient classical civilizations otherwise we are victims of an oppressed history. Diop claims that:

> Les processus de revolution des langues africaines apparait clarement; loin de nous comprenons que le walaf descende par filiation directe de l'egyptien ancien, mais le walaf, l'egyptien et les

autres langues africaines derivent d'une langue mere commune que l'on peut appeler le paleo-africain.[26]

Diop explains further that the comparison of languages, particularly at the lexical level, would permit the elimination of false etymologies. He believes that the mother language, this Diopian paleo-African language, can be shown to be common to most African languages, including ancient Egyptian. He establishes this thesis in the comprehensive and substantive *Parente Genetique de L'Egyptien Pharaonique et des Langues Negro-Africaines* published in 1977.[27]

Unquestionably, the graphic systems of Africa, whether carved in stone, written on papyrus, formed out of objects, or shaped in the sand, represent enormous variations and complexity. In the sacred writing of ancient Egypt we see the beginning of knowledge about ourselves, about Africa, indeed, about the world because the anteriority of Egypt in graphic systems has meaning for the whole world since our entry into history is through the open door of the Nile River.

AFRICAN NAMES AND CONCEPTS AS DISSEMINATED

We find not only the origins of monumental civilization in Africa but also the linguistic basis for many Hebrew and Christian names. Moses, for example, the name of the greatest Hebrew prophet, is derived from the ancient Kemetic *msi* "to give birth," *msw* which is found in the Kemetic names *Thothmoses* "begotten of Thoth," and *Rameses* "begotten of Ra." On this point it should be noted that in Yoruba the Kemetic *msi* occurs as *misi* as in oyo *misi,* the title of the kingmakers at Oyo. They are "begotten at Oyo," descendants of the soil.

Furthermore, there is some support for the view that *amen* first occurs in the pharaonic names such as Amenhotep, Amenomope, and Tutankhamen. Thus, the Arabic, Hebrew and Greek use of *amen* as a denouement to a praise or prayer has its base in the ancient Egyptian name for the deity, Amen. In Turkish the word *Amin* carries a meaning similar to that of *Amen* in Arabic, Hebrew, and Greek, but "Aman" is an exclamation that expresses shock and a cry for divine intervention. Both of these meanings may hark back to the ancient African deity as well. Used in Turkish to ask for forgiveness, "Aman" seeks to beg mercy from God or Allah in a desperate situation.

In view of the persistent attacks on African culture from the point of alphabetism, which is the valorization of writing as preferable to any other system of communication, it has been my intention to do two things: (1) to demonstrate that writing is not the only way to transmit culture and knowledge, and (2) to demonstrate that there is no intrinsic value in writing which constitutes a "superior" stage of evolution. The correct presentation of African graphic developments suggests that, if anything, writing began on the continent of Africa. Nevertheless, one should not assume from that position either any superiority of writing.

Preiswerk and Perrot have made a valuable contribution by writing, "teaching the alphabet is obviously not ethnocentric in itself; however, the hypothesis of the universal value of literacy, conferring on it the quality of quasi-absolute objective is questionable in view of other needs of a society and its economy."

I shall now turn to the discussion of the rhetorical power of Ma'at and its relationship to the practical level of human speech. Since classical African civilization in Kemet was suspended from the twin beams of literature and orature, our intellectual interest should lead to the sanguine possibilities of understanding African philosophy and language from an Afrocentric perspective rather than an anemic dismissal of the search for peace and harmony as might be the case in some European circles.

THE RHETORICAL POWER OF MA'AT

Maulana Karenga has written in *Selections from the Husia* that "Husia" signifies "the two divine powers by which Ra created the world, i.e., 'Hu,' authoritative utterance, and 'Sia,' exceptional insight."[28] Rhetoric, the theory of authoritative utterance, and oratory, elegant utterance, is intricately related to Egyptian life. In fact, despite the significance of the hieroglyphic, hieratic and demotic scripts that have given us so much information about ancient Africa, the Egyptians were primarily an oral people. Even the transmittal of the dead to the spirit world was accompanied by the spoken word. It is therefore no wonder that the Egyptians conceived of the concerns of oratory, the functions of rhetoric, and the nature of the systematic investigation of both the practice of public speaking, oratory, and its theory, rhetoric.

Reference to primary texts, however, provides us with our evidences since the spoken word was not preserved in ancient time. Actually, *The Coming Forth by* Day is itself a veritable expression of Egyptian style and rhetorical disposition. If we examined the canons of oratory established by the Egyptians under the tutelage of Djehuti, the lord of divine speech, we will have the fundamental categories for oratory as contemporary as a Barack Obama, Malcolm X or Martin Luther King, Jr. For example, the origin of the introductory salutation is found in the *t'etet,* oratorical expression of "adoration of Ra who rises in the eastern skies." The aim of such a salutation is to open a public speech. It was later made by the Hebrews and Arabs introductions such as "to the God of Abraham, Isaac and Jacob" or "in the name of Allah, the most merciful."

Based on the historically correct position of Africans, the introductory salutations were intended to connect the present audience to the past. The speaker, in this case, was a nexus for the past and present. In order for an orator to perform at the highest levels he had to know the special duties of the speaker that related to Ma'at. No orator could effectively speak with Djehuti's eloquence unless he understood the special character of Ma'at.

"Know thyself!" the admonition written on the temple at Kar-

nak, reverberated deep in the heart of the ancient Egyptian orator. After the union of the two kingdoms, the Egyptians attained
a high degree of knowledge of their material surroundings. They
had erected pyramids, carved sphinxes, graded roads, introduced
geometry, studied the stars, and built beautiful temples. By 2400
B.C. the last great pyramids had been built. And yet it is not only
the monumental material contributions of ancient Egypt that at-
tract our attention. Egypt was always in search of immortality.
In fact, immortality is the principal theme of its massive temples
and pyramids. The quest for wisdom and truth occupied the lives
of the elders but it was also a quest actively pursued by initiates
who knew it as the pathway to establishing the proper order. Life
was meaningless without this order. Consequently the priests
as orators exercised considerable control over the philosophical
thoughts of the society as they performed official duties at the
temples. It was their voices that woke the deities in the morning
and put them to sleep at night.

In South Africa it is said that one of the Nguni priests sat for
a long time in complete silence in the presence of his students.
When the students showed some uneasiness at the silence the old
priest said, "If yesterday's lesson suggests no questions we have no
starting point for today's lessons." Whatever the initiate studied,
nothing was so important as achieving total knowledge of self. Let
me explain. The Egyptian gods gave no divine guidance. Henri
Frankfort says that the gods were known to require that "a person

respect Ma'at but there were no specific divine commands which shaped human action."[29] What we know is that it was considered "right" to maintain unity of heart and tongue, conviction and speech, "right" to respect authority and right to enjoy inheritance. Yet human wisdom alone gave direction, there were no directives from gods. The whole oratorical enterprise was one that followed the signposts of the sages and sought not struggle or confrontation but harmony and balance in speech and behavior.

On the whole, even when a person erred it was not conceived of as rebellion against god. The person did not commit a crime against god; the person was moving against the established order and the responsibility of one god or another was to see that the order was vindicated. In Egypt as throughout Africa there is no violent conflict between gods and humans; there is also no image of the individual hero. The concept "the wrath of God" does not appear either and consequently the aberrations of the Egyptians are not sinful as against god; they are the results of ignorance and the poor fellow must be disciplined. The truly ignorant knows neither good nor evil. Such a person violates the principles of Ma'at. Ignorant orators are violators of Ma'at, bringers of disharmony.

Although the book, *The Coming Forth by Day,* often called *The Book of the Dead,* deals with passage from life to death, in its deeper meaning it is a book about Ma'at. Ma'at, when applied to public speaking is the product of existential tension. A speaker achieves it only when he self-consciously knows that he is indeed alive.

Ma'at, ultimately a spiritual concept, is the central notion in the questing life. Yet an orator can only become truly Ma'at oriented in the company of a thousand gods. The one is not separated from the other, and the other cannot exist without the one. A speaker needs an audience. In fact, it is only by the heart of Ausar in us that we can become Ma'at-oriented. What is it then?

Ma'at is a social, ethical, and rhetorical term. The Egyptians understood it as the divine order of creation, of society, of nature. Since the cosmos was one they had no difficulty with Ma'at meaning justice, truth, harmony; the categories and contrasts are ours. Even today in traditional African societies medicine, ethics, and rhetoric are connected. In the West one may believe that nature is cruel and that belief does not affect anything else. This is not true in Africa. All things are connected. Among the Yoruba, a child is not a person until the name is spoken.

Ma'at becomes a symbol of the search for existential peace, it preserves whatever union with the Egyptian "deep sources" are necessary to reveal the modalities of the spirit which manifest truth, justice, and wisdom. Everything in rhetorical expression reveals unity between the person and the cosmos. This cosmos is a unified spiritual totality different from the materialized universe of a technocratic perspective that does not yield cosmos. In effect, Ma'at apprehends spirit in matter. There is no oppositional clement in the spiritual and material as in the western oppositions of body/mind, knowledge/opinion, male/female, science/religion, and so on. To the Egyptian the cosmos had complementary pairs. That is why the divine being in most African cultures following Egypt is androgynous, therefore able to reproduce itself. Thus, the orator searches for harmony in conflict.

The African view is little changed from this idea of unity with the cosmos. In the sense of the Zulu declaration, one says, "I am river, I am mountain, **I am** tree, I am love, I am emotion, I am beauty, I am lake, I am cloud, I am sun, I am sky, I am mind, I am one with one." There is no difference between human beings in knowledge-of-themselves and the *cosmos-becoming*. The symbols that suggest Ma'at provide existential connections to those who would decipher the orator's message, the dancer's dance, the drummer's rhythms, and the healer's power, axé.

Ma'at's special character seems to have been righteousness and rightness in the person. Justice, truth, and righteousness were often used to denote Ma'at. Righteousness is more that the rightness we find in nature, however: righteousness is a transpersonal experience within the human order. One cannot be righteous because it is a continuous process by which we align ourselves with the harmony we find in nature. Thus, righteousness is a dynamic process and when we say "be righteous" we only mean it as a process for the moment, for the particular context. One may have integrity but one cannot have righteousness.

The performer's search for *soul* becomes a search for cosmic unity. Like the entire enterprise of the death mystery in the Egyptian pyramid narratives oratory, dance, music, medicine are efforts to address the cosmic union. One merges with the past and in this merging with the past finds the pathway to the future. There is no discovery, no transpersonal insight, without according the past its proper place. This is why the most advanced psychotherapies attempt to have a person make peace with the past in a quest for present and future peace. The ancient Egyptians understood this and endeavored to ritualize the transpersonal experience by using symbolic representations of the experience. One travels as Ra travels and emerges as Ra emerges. The dead person is committed to the "womb" of the *mir*, pyramid, much like the initiate is made to remain in an isolated cabin, prior to receiving qualifications to enter into life. Therefore, the ancient Egyptian, as other African peoples, did not carry on a widespread practice of cremation. The aim was to have the person emerge as whole. The womb, the tomb, and the encapsulating process of searching for Ma'at in the closet of the mind as the body is secluded from the community become symbols of the quest for righteousness. The basis for all art and performance, including oratory is found in this questing life.

Akhenaten's heresy, after thousands of years of the Egyptian attempt for harmony through Ma'at working internally, was that he sought in Aten the one cosmic generator that gave meaning to life. But this force, this one god heresy, was external, outside of the individual, a cosmic weaver weaving from afar. Thus, Akhenaten's heresy was not the elevation of Aten as the only god force, nor the

de-emphasis of Ptah, Horus, Set, Nut, Osiris, Khnemu, or Djehuti, but the replacement of the individual's quest for Ma'at with
a giver or chief of Ma'at. The worship of the solar disk, *solarism*,
reached its zenith under Akhenaten (Amenhotep IV) because he
prohibited the worship of all gods except the great disk of the sun.
He ordered the names of other gods erased from monuments and
called Amen Ra by the name Aten in an unsuccessful effort to
replace the Almighty. One hymn to Amen-Ra goes "Adoration to
thee, O Amen-Ra, the bull in Annu, the ruler of all the gods, the
beautiful and beloved god who gives life by means of every kind
of food and fine cattle." This hymn, itself rhetorical, was meant to
serve rhetorical ends. Akhenaten attempted to appropriate such
hymns for Aten in direct challenge to the priests at Waset.

Furthermore, the priests of Waset say, "You are chief of all the
gods, lord of Ma'at, father of the gods, creator of men and women,
maker of beasts and cattle, lord of all that exists ...." Ma'at becomes
under the heresy of Akhenaten a possession of Aten when before
throughout the search for the transcendental state the initiate had
relied upon self-consciousness produced by following a knowledge
of causes. Initiates were never principal priests or orators. They
took their cues from those who possessed experienced *kas,* the
priests, who evoked consciousness that transcended disharmonies.

The ancient Egyptian quest for Ma'at was not linear and based
on acquisition of technology but on the certitude that could only
come from an understanding of causes. There again is the impera-

tive to the student "know thyself!" The uncovering of the inner
ear is the first requirement for being a good orator. Only through
knowledge of causes can the person achieve harmony, otherwise
disorder and disharmony, which represent evil, dominate. Whenever disorder exists in the individual or between the individual
and nature, we have the concept of evil, the equivalent of the exis-
tentialist's indecisiveness, the only sin. In African thought, disharmony in the community must be quickly corrected. This is why
there was often a dependence on the consecration made to the
vital function that a particular animal incarnated. We sometimes
speak of animal worship that, by the way, occurs nowhere that I
know of in Africa. There are rhythmic meditations that were used
to clarify essential functions of nature. This was not a worship of
animals, but a grasping for essentiality, that which was necessary
for the right functioning of society. As modern Europeans and
Americans sacrifice humans in athletics or in war the classical African relationship with the universe was to demonstrate that the
sacrifice of animals was a demonstration of humility before the
universe. What was the society willing to do to recreate the harmony that had been shattered by human beings? How would the
people re-orient themselves after crisis? How shall we be ushered
into being again, that is, once more?

The scarab, the oval, and a kneeling man with a wave over his
head represent the expression "I shall come into existence." Thus
spoke Ra and therein is the secret to the orator's objective. What

we reach for is the source of harmony with nature, to be absorbed in the flow of the cosmos; that is the life the ancient Egyptians understood. Throughout the papyrus of Ani one finds the question, "What is it then?" The answer to this repeated question is various but in the end the message of harmony between humans and nature is clear. "I cackle as a goose, I fly as a hawk." In other words, I am one with nature. In fact if the orator's senses are trained by the laws of Ma'at, then the orator is able to master appearance and function.

The choice of an animal as a symbol was not random. The priests did not go out and choose the first creature that came along to represent digestion but they chose the jackal. This animal kills its prey, buries it and returns to eat it when it has begun to decompose. It becomes a symbol for digestion, physical and metaphysical. We observe life, growth, death, coagulation, decomposition and transformation. No being can begin the process of rebirth until its form has disintegrated. All methods of reaching the mind understand this technically. Rhetoric is no different. The jackal-headed Anubis always led the soul of the deceased into the first stage of the dwat, world of transformations. When the body of the deceased was mummified, the organs were removed, dehydrated, and placed in urns. The urn containing the intestines has a jackal on it, suggesting the connection between the intestines and digestion. The jackal gives life through that which is poison for others. The destructive process of digestion becomes an element in transformation. The jackal must dig up his buried morsels at the proper time or they may pass into an indigestible state of chaos.

Ma'at reveals itself through the spoken word and sculpted images. A sign is often "hollowed out to signify entering into matter; it is in relief, when leaving it is signified." In certain ways the tombs show this, the entry being the placing of the body into the earth; the exit being the resurrection, the rise and fall of the Nile, the ebb and flow of our existence.

Rhetoric becomes a counterweight that evaluates the heart of the living as Ma'at evaluates the dead. Ma'at is symbolized by a feather, and is present in the weighing process. In such a case, a heart on a plate of balance is counterweighted by a feather representing Ma'at. The plummet or weight attached to a line represents the emotional life of a person. Ma'at has two dimensions, one is divine and the other is the individual Ma'at whom the dead should have realized in him or herself. Ma'at is cosmic consciousness, universal ideation, essential wisdom, proceeding ceaselessly from divine Ra, whose nourishment she is. A teacher is most successful when the student has a unifying vision. An orator is effective when he creates a union with his audience.

Our knowledge of the symbol is always limited. We can never know all aspects of the symbol. It is unlimited, infinite. There is no person who could know all the possibilities of a symbol. It would mean innate knowledge of the entire universe. Ma'at does not mean that, it does not imply that, but rather it suggests knowledge of self as the absolute path to knowledge of symbols. This knowledge is constructive, liberating, knowledge of synthesis as opposed to a rational, analytical knowledge which dismantles and destroys. Ma'at becomes a way to a new state of thought, a transpersonal opening of our intelligence. But this takes simplicity of heart-mind as opposed to complexity; synthesis as opposed to analysis.

Ogotemmeli, the Dogon priest, reveals to Marcel Griaule during a thirty-day interview that the Dogon people of Mali know that the time has come when secret things must be said.[30] The Dogon knew that intuitive sensations held the mysterious call to knowledge. Spirit-energy, soul dominates matter and matter may be a temporary phenomenon anyway, particularly in its relationship to life. When the body is dead, life is thought to be transcendental to matter and independent of the physical and chemical laws that govern matter. The Egyptians did not put it just that way but they understood that Ma'at, the ultimate cause, did not operate wholly within the framework of material laws. The images, symbols, found in the temples and tombs were only representative of the innate knowledge and absolute truth that existed apart from the material.

There is a verse in the Ifa divination of the Yoruba which reads *ologbon kan o to koko omi seti aso* or "no wise person can tie water into a knot." Ma'at is like this. It is not subject to the whims of outside forces, it exists within a person. We must find it in ourselves, flowing forward harmoniously. This is the lesson of the ancient Africans.

Interdependence and reciprocity are seen in ritual sacrifice. As the ultimate philosophic expression, ritual serves to provide symbolic truth to our relationship with Ma'at. We die and are reborn through symbols and the light as a feather symbol of Ma'at, the judge of our heart, revitalizes us. Rhetoric is preeminently theory about the use of symbols.

The African American knows "this little light of mine" shines because of Ma'at although the sentiment is appropriated for something entirely different. We are eternally being born in the affirmation of life. As testaments to the abiding influence of the classical Africans we celebrate the affirmation of a judgment rendered in our favor. Ma'at judgment validates our inner work for harmony and humanness.

Let us understand. The cause is seen through the effect. Observation of a concrete symbol of a fact helps to evoke its abstraction. Throughout the Egyptian myth there is a knowledge of the successive appearance of divine properties which have emerged from the original unity where these properties are in a latent state—then there is a knowledge of these properties in the continuous creation where they are made known by nature. It is possible to speak of the ne_ters, gods of Egypt, as a "hierarchy of the neteru (_neters_)," much like in the later Hindu or Hebrew *kabbala,* but in one important way this hierarchy of the gods is unlike those traditions—it is not "dogmatized." The neteru (_neters_) do not have a hierarchy based on their appearance as primary or secondary causes and do not have a hierarchy based on the nature of their function, spiritual, or material. The Egyptians, like other Africans, have scattered the elements of knowledge, and one has to fit them together like a puzzle in order to know the picture.

Ma'at is the cumulative appearances of the divine properties. I smell a flower and say "wonderful." I am surely at that moment full of wonder. A myriad of experiences, all connected to the latent unity, work the miracle of Ma'at for us as we either speak or hear spoken the golden words of Djehuti. There is something that transcends myth; Ma'at is truth in all things, the reason of life, the purpose of speech, and the source of happiness. Nature itself gives us the concrete meanings to abstractions; it reveals symbolic forms and expressions that may be spoken. That is why no access to the "keys" of this knowledge will help us unless we adopt our way of seeing to the simplicity of spiritual synthesis.

There are few African myths of the universe emerging out of chaos. Harmony preexists chaos; it comes before confusion and turmoil, and is in itself, in the African view, the original condition. Whether you study the ancient Kemetic view or the various derivatives of that view you find that harmony is at the center of existence. The Yoruba claim that it was after Orunmila had done his great works that his children on earth brought about confusion. Yoruba is only one of the great traditions that emphasize the concept of harmony out of which the world began.

Ma'at functions as the celebration of harmony and balance in the life of African people. While I may refer to various myths from African history, it is important that we do not confuse myths with theologies, philosophies, or ideologies. Myths are tales. They are not meant to provide a systematic treatment of theology, philosophy, or ideology, but they give us explanations of origins in the form of tales. Therefore I shall use the ancient Kemetic conception of Ma'at as a point of departure in a discussion of the African way against injustice. But those are analyses developed with the idea of bringing to the fore a fundamental idea rooted in African culture. What a systematic account, such as I propose here, will do is to demonstrate organic connectives to African culture in continental and Diasporan African areas.

In pursuit of this connective I shall examine, first and in brief outline, the idea of Ma'at in Kemet, Ma'at in African commonalities, and the transformation of Ma'atic ideas in the Diaspora. Certainly I recognize that this in and of itself is not enough in methodological terms, so I endeavor to establish a methodological direction, that is, how do Afrocentrists arrive at a Ma'atic condition in contemporary society. My work in this regard is in deference to the monumental volume by my colleague, Maulana Karenga, *Maat: The Moral Ideal in Ancient Kemet*, and my former student, Willie Cannon-Brown's, *Nefer: The Aesthetic Ideal in Ancient Egypt*, a work that that is inspired by the example of Karenga's pioneering book. With these works we have opened new doors to the power of African ideas. Much of what I will write in succeeding pages owes conception to Karenga mostly, and to Cannon-Brown.[31]

Ma'at is sometimes called the Kemetic quality of "order," "justice," "righteousness," and "balance." Karenga has identified seven traits that are translated into English for Ma'at. He names them as truth order, justice, righteousness, balance, harmony, and reciprocity. Each of these terms is important in understanding the concept, yet neither one is sufficient in and of itself. Ma'at is a vast ocean and there are many waves that constitute its meaning. Indeed Ma'at may be seen as a cosmic element similar in its energy to Axé in Yoruba. Eshu is able to maintain balance and order in society by the use of Axé. We are correct if we see Ma'at as the ruling force between good and evil. When you speak of it as the organizing principle of human society, the creative spirit of phenomena, and the eternal order of the universe, you come close to understanding what the ancient Kemetic civilization understood.

The permutations of the Kemetic concept may be found in numerous other cultures. For example, the Old English word for measure is "Maeth," the Dutch word for measure is "Maat" and the Amharic word for balance is "Meezan." Furthermore, the West African language of Hausa use the expression "Ma'aunu" for measuring scales. In Kemet, the philosophers understood "Maakheru" to indicate to be justified. The word "mathematics" finds its source in the ancient Kemetic Ma'at through the Greek "Mathematikos" and the Latin "Mathematicus." Both the Greek and the Latin words use the ancient stem "Mathe" which carries the meaning of precision and exactness. In this sense they are related to the Kemetic idea of measure. Lacking an imperialistic ethos, Kemet did not spread its concepts by force of arms like Rome or Islam but by the practical use of the idea.

This idea of Ma'at is the idea of justice not merely in legal terms but in terms of the proper relationship between a human person and the universe, between the person and nature, between the person and another person. Thus, Ma'at means that which is perfectly established, fixed in the position of good because it possesses the quality of a force, energy that regulates the relationship of the universe. So the kings of Egypt were not merely kings, they were the embodiment of the concept of Ma'at, and the goddess Ma'at stood with them so long as they stood with Ma'at. They did not have empirical testing and quantification of the type often thought of today; they had evidence of the truth in the proper relationship of things, in the propriety of human beings to the order maintained by the gods. Therefore, our understanding of Ma'at in the Kemetic tradition is predicated on our appreciation for the concept of order, measure, limit, and form, that is, form in the sense of order and justice. Ma'at confirmed the stability of society and nature. If one looks at the later Greek derivations, we see that the Greeks took the Kemetic traditions and misunderstood them. George James, in *Stolen Legacy,* tells us that there is no Greek philosophy, only stolen African philosophy.

The Greeks, particularly Pythagoras and Heraclitus, took the Kemetic idea of Ma'at and attempted to change it into mathematics. Aristotle says that the followers of Pythagoras devoted themselves to mathematics as if it constituted the only form. They said that things consisted of numbers. Many descendants of Pythagoras still believe this strange doctrine. It should be pointed out, however, that Pythagoras came to this view for religious reasons.

Affected by the Kemetic teachings on the immortality of the soul, Pythagoras sought to utilize as much of the priestly teachings of Kemet as he could in the development of his own views. He reached into Africa for some sense of reality since the Homeric gods were not real gods as far as he was concerned. They were just like human beings. He wanted something that was different, perhaps distant and more remote from humans than the Homeric gods. Homeric gods could neither inspire others nor be the objects of worship. The religion of Dionysus, borrowed from ancient Kemet, had satisfied some of the Greek yearning for transcendence in the seventh century B.C. but this was a caricature of Kemetic religion. The Dionysians often worked themselves into frenzy and exhausted themselves drinking wine mixed with animal blood.

Pythagoras rebelled against this as pagan and introduced the idea of a spectator who sits back and observes life. Thus, the Greek word "theory" means also to "look on." I think that Pythagoras' idea of form by which he meant "limit" in a numerical sense was an attempt to re-recreate the Kemetic Ma'at in secular terms. For Pythagoras harmony is the form that the limiting structure of numerical ratio imposes upon the unlimited possibilities for sounds with the strings of a musical instrument. In medicine he saw the same principle at work. Health was the harmony or balance or proper ratio of certain opposites such as hot and cold, wet and dry, and various other elements. But these concepts are found in the Kemetic idea that health is only possible when the body is "in tune" with nature. In every African society the same principle adheres. The difference is that the Greeks wanted to quantify this—how many, how much.

Maat reigned supreme among the ancient Kemetic people for at least two millennia before they heard of the Greeks. It was Heraclitus who introduced to the Greeks the terms flux and unity. All things were in flux and therefore you cannot step in the same river twice. Things are forever changing. This idea of flux is applied to everything, including the soul. Thus in the sixth century B.C. Heraclitus was grappling with the concept of balance by introducing the idea of flux. But this was a particularistic notion, not holistic, and very much like Anaximenes' notion that air was the key to everything because it was everywhere. One day the Greeks thought the key was air, the next day they said it was fire; then they said it was earth or water, when in fact the Kemetians recognized that these were all interactive concepts. They operated in relationship to each other.

Throughout the history of Kemet, even when Tuthmosis III bestrode the world as the greatest known conqueror in the world, and down to the reigns of Pianki and Tarharka, the idea of order and justice was incorporated in the total relationship of the Universe, all things were connected. Ma'at encapsulated the idea of rightness. In fact, Tuthmosis instructions to his vizier Rekhmire were etched into the wall of Rekhmire's tomb. In the wall paintings Ma'at was personified as Ma'at, the goddess; Ma'at was the feather balanced against the heart of a dead person to check that the candidates for entry to heaven could truly claim to be free of evil; Ma'at stood in judgment as a living goddess; Ma'at was a proper behavior towards others, towards nature; Ma'at was a pragmatic approach to moral or ethical life. In the words of Tuthmosis III, "Look to the office of vizier. It sustains the lands. When a petitioner comes from Upper or Lower Kemet see that everything done conforms to the spirit of the law. A petitioner should not say, 'My right has been denied me.' The god hates partiality; treat the person you know equally with the person you do not. Let men respect you because you offer justice. This is laid upon you."

MA'AT IN AFRICAN COMMONALITIES

A fundamental position of my argument is that all African societies find Kemet a common source for intellectual and philosophical ideas. These manifestations are shown, for example, in: the conversations of the Dogon's blind philosopher Ogotommeli;

Zulu oral poetry, as brought to us by Mazisi Kunene; Yoruba Ifa divination instructions and efficacy; Nsibidi texts and their emphasis on balance; an in the practices and words of the Shona *mhondoros*, spirit mediums. Wole Soyinka, the Nigerian Nobel Laureate for Literature, has argued that African culture is one and that the idea of a unity of African culture is not to be looked upon as retrogressive. This is the position I take with respect to the dissemination of the Ma'atic concept throughout the African world.

There are five Kemetic concepts that constitute the Ma'atic response to injustice and disorder in the world. Those concepts must be seen in the light of general African cultural developments. You cannot separate Kemet from an understanding of the basic ideas in Baganda, Udok, Kikuyu or Dinka. For this reason I have gone to the idea of Ma'at in search of its manifestations in the Kemetic tradition and have tried to see how those traditions appear in other parts of the African world. Certainly there are differences in response based upon environmental conditions and other factors but I believe that the general cultural project against chaos represented by Ma'at with an *ankh* in her hand is encompassed by my classification, using five Kemetic concepts: *tep, pet, heb, sen*, and *meh*.

Tep (Beginning)

   Love of Children Late Weaning

   Age-grouping

   Value Fertility

Pet (Extensions)

    Society above Individual Extended Family

    Honor to Ancestors

Heb (Festival)

    Agricultural Rites

    Art for Ritual

    Dance/Music

    Gift-Giving

    Ceremony for Passages Ululations

Sen (Circle)

    Burial

    Extended Funeral Living Ancestors

Meh (Crowning Glory)

    Supreme Deity

    Search for Harmony (Ma'at) Freedom from Shame

The transformation of these concepts throughout Africa and the African world has meant that the influence of Kemet continues unabated even in the language and behavior of Africans in the Americas and Caribbean. We are essentially a people of Ma'at, we cannot escape it because it is based upon thousands of years of history. C. Tsehloane Keto told the story of a European missionary who had great difficulty with a man in southern Africa whom he was trying to convert. He asked the man if he had sinned, the man being more than sixty-five years old. The African responded to the

European that he had not sinned. Confused, the European said, "You cannot live so long without sinning because to not sin at your age is impossible." Of course, the African answered, "Your term sin refers to you and your beliefs, not to me." Therein is the problem the African may have committed many acts that the European may have called sins but in the Ma'atic formulation whenever he had done so he had corrected the balance, he had performed the rituals that would have restored the balance. Therefore, he had not sinned in his tradition or in the Europeans because the right ordering of relationships, the performance of the necessary rites re-establishes the justness of the society. Furthermore, the question of sinning was not an African question and this created confusion as well. Totally abandoning the African collective idea of shame the European reached for the individualistic guilt-ridden idea of sinning.

Among the Sotho and the Xhosa all order begins with human beings existing in a state of order internally and externally. The proper kind of relationship to the universe is one of balance, rhythm, circularity, and justness. The idea of evil resides in the ability of a person to "mess around with" the natural order, to tamper with the state of harmony. But evil is always associated with human beings; it does not, and cannot exist apart from some human touch. Once evil is found to be present and human beings appear to be in a state of confusion because of it, then there has to be a ritual to make it right, to rebalance the natural order. The

Ma'atic force is always greater than evil force.

Almost every human activity that involves a negative action that causes the balance to be lost must be dealt with through some form of cleansing. If a person accidentally kills someone that person must be cleansed. Purification is essential to the restoration of balance. Armies that go into battle and struggle with opposing armies must have purification ceremonies before and after battle. War is the epitome of society in turmoil. Cleansing is essential for soldiers. Thus, even in contemporary times, such as with the Second Chimurenga struggle for Zimbabwe in the 1970s until independence, the soldiers were cleansed and blessed by the spirit medium Nehanda before they went into battle. All of this is related to balance. It cannot be escaped that wholeness, integrity, security, and justice are related to the idea of restoring harmony.

Ma'at is the fundamental reality, without it there is no understanding, no harmony, and no possible restoration of balance. Otherwise we become like isolated satellites without power or direction drifting into space. Ma'at imposes order and direction, gives us a true and adequate meaning of our life and is the major force against chaos. God does not hold the world on his shoulders as the Greeks believed but she, as the goddess Ma'at, keeps the universe from disorder. The king, though a god, could not rule arbitrarily. Like all things in the universe even the king was subject to Ma'at.

Ma'at was the incantation of truth and justice, but more than that because it was the cosmic principle of harmony. But Africans have continued to say that you cannot have harmony without truth and justice. The Kemetic idea was to represent Ma'at as a charming figure, wearing an ostrich plume on her head and often holding an ankh. The vizier, the Supreme Judge of Kemet, was the Priest of Ma'at. He served her primary interest in keeping chaos from entering the sanctuary of order. Nothing was more important than putting truth in the place of falsity, maintaining harmony's strength over conflict, and righting wrong in the nature of things. Everything was affected. If a vase was on its side, you righted it; if a staff fell to the ground from its position against the wall, you stood it up again. Thus, every act of protocol was connected to Ma'at; all decency, courtesies, and habits of cleanliness were related to Ma'at. This diminutive figure of Ma'at represented the concept of Ma'at as all-inclusive and all-forceful, that is, in the language of force. The original force field was the concept of Ma'at. Amenhotep III put the conviction of the kings best when he said that his whole aim was to make Kemet blossom as it had in "primeval times" by means of Ma'at. This is a powerful statement of purpose.

The cosmos regulated all of its constituents and these parts were organic to each other. In their relationship they constituted a perfect order. Included in this perfection were the human being, the heavenly bodies, the change of seasons, the rising and setting of the sun, the yearly overflowing of the Nile, and the maintenance of a stable society. When a king was Ma'atic, the people were secure, and their trust in their government was assured. Security, therefore, in life and death, in social order and cosmic order, was reaffirmed forever from the moment of creation by the enactment of ritual.

There is both continuity and circularity in this idea of Ma'at. The principle of eternal recurrence is central to the Kemetic world-view. That is why it is impossible to separate the beginning from the crowning glory but rather to see them as constant re-enactments of the truth of order. We help to hold the world together through ritual observance. Ultimately that is what we are doing when we turn a behavior into a rite. The Eurocentric idea of straightforward progression in time from beginning to end did not occur in Kemetic thought. African thought was in terms of cycles, circles, and hence, a cosmic continuity. When a king took the throne, he reaffirmed Ma'at. His ascension signified that he returned to the everlasting beginnings of the cosmic order and thus kept it going by his divinity. It is this circularity that is at the heart of the concept of kingship in all African societies. One may easily confuse the Eurocentric idea of the divine rights with the African idea of the king as expressive of Ma'atic continuity. One leads to formulations like that expressed by the caesars, the emperors, or the Russian czars, in which a person can claim to be anything he wants to be. This is a very individualistic concept. Different czars possessed different attitudes toward their duties and offices and had different directions in their reigns, but the Kemetic ruler was in fact the embodiment of something eternal, something superior to the hold of the office. This is the relationship of the Oba, the Alafin, and the king of Baganda to reality; this is an underlying commonality in African societies.

CHAPTER THREE

Confronting The Historical Situation

Interrogating African Culture

Afrocentric scholars have searched for a method that would illuminate the role of African culture in advancing human society. The task for method, however, is enormous because it must admit an approach that takes into consideration many African cultures, the dissemination of Kemetic ideas, and the closeting of certain rituals behind esoteric ceremonies as the priests responded to foreign encroachments. None of this is impossible. But as the Akan say, "the person who can untie this knot knows the secret of the *dja*." The Baule people of Ivory Coast have always understood the *dja* to be the core of human life and existence. What is more important for us than the exploration of our own minds? This is why the questions of existence have always been at the base of African cultural life.

Niangoran-Bouah's book, *The Akan World of Gold Weights*, is a most valuable advance in our approach to Maat. The whole idea of *dja* is close to Maat. The *dja* is not merely gold-weights but the Akan concept of order, balance, fairness, justice. Niangoran-Bouah says the *dja* dates back to the beginning of time. While all elements of the *dja*, figurative and geometrical, are weights, they represent the sacred, special place of the idea in African society. The word *adja*, heritage, for example, comes from the word *dja*. One's *dja* is passed on to a relative at death. But *dja* is a concept, a philosophical concept that goes beyond the mere idea of weights; it is a Maatic concept with the aspects of balance, justice, fairness, and integrity playing a major role in our understanding of it. One is not just dealing with gold-weights when one discusses *dja*; one is also encountering Maat in its Akan manifestation. The father or mother who dies may pass the *dja* to a son or daughter. It is this power that allows the receiver to have ritual energy.

What is true of Akan is also true of Yoruba. Ifa, or Orunmila, is the spirit of divination among the Yoruba, but that is not the end of Ifa. The priest of Ifa, the Babalawo, is the one who has the secret. What is the secret that is held by Babalawo? It is the eso-teric knowledge through which he can open the future and learn the wish of Ifa. Thus when a child is born, when a marriage is proposed, when laying the foundations of a town, or when making war or making peace, one consults with Ifa. The reason this is so is because Ifa is Maatic, that is, Ifa serves to reestablish the balances that have been destroyed or to prevent the harmony from descending into conflict. One cannot believe in Maat and not understand that Ifa comes from the same source. Ancient Kemet stands to Yoruba, Akan, Shona, and African Americans like the step pyramid (*mr*) of Zoser stands in relationship to all other pyramids, first and prototypical. This is the basic philosophical perspective on method.

There are four elementary considerations in the attempt to establish a method for assuring the ascendancy of Maat:

- The Unity of Occasion/Situation
- The Elimination of Chaos
- The Elevation of Peace among Disparate Voices
- The Creation of Harmony and Balance

Any text or person in action may be examined from these elementary considerations. The establishment of Maat and the Maatic principles, which now we can claim to be not a world-view but more correctly a world voice, rests upon these four columns of analysis.

A person who seeks the road to Maat must come by the column of unity. This, of course, is no miracle because consciousness precedes unity. The person who wants to analyze anything for the purpose of synthesis will find that the first rule is to examine the object, thing, person, speech for unity. As Afrocentrists, that is our first obligation because it is the first step on the road to Maat. If a person, objects, thing, or book seek to eliminate chaos, that is also on the path to Maat. We tell by the thematic choice, the treatment of that choice, and the resolution of a problem whether the elimination for chaos was important for the person or not.

Peace is not the absence of struggle. In truth sometimes peace is only found in struggle. But the elevation of peace, predicated on justice and fairness, can be identified as Maatic. You can examine any person or occasion for the qualities of peace. There are always people who misunderstand peace-loving for weakness, but the Maatic world voice shows the search for peace to be one way to tell if a person or document is on the proper pathway.

Harmony is the final stage of Maat; it is the African way against injustice and chaos. We arrive at it through the integrity of ideas, without shame, and of course, without guilt since guilt is unknown in traditional African culture. Shame is the moral enforcer in African culture; guilt is a European individualistic concept.

ON SIGNS AND SYMBOLS

Several nineteenth and twentieth century European writers thought to place Africa in its anterior place by writing meaningful, though sometimes flawed, accounts of African origin. Albert

Churchward was one such writer. Mary Lefkowitz' *Not Out of Africa* was a diatribe against Afrocentric thinkers and the early white scholars who had argued for the superior position of African culture. She claims that writers such as Churchward were freemasons who confused the nature of ancient Egypt and unwittingly gave a boost to Afrocentric thinking. Of course, Lefkowitz got it wrong and in several debates with her I pointed out that ancient Kemet existed before the creation of the freemasons and that all human building, particularly stone masonry, started with Africa. Nevertheless, European writers began to appropriate ancient Egypt and attempt to make it a part of European heritage. While we can appreciate some of these works and their opinions and analyses we must be clear that their interests are often contrary to African interests. Yet Churchward's contributions must be seen in the light of its time.

Albert Churchward's massive work on *The Signs and Symbols of Primordial Man,* first published in 1913, came as a shock to the keepers of what Martin Bernal calls the Aryan model. There were several major contributions presented by Churchward: (1) the African origin of signs and symbols, (2) the diffusion of African symbolism to the Pacific and Central America, and (3) the debt freemasonry owed to Africans. In fact, Churchward proved long before Mary Lefkowitz' attack against African origins that freemasonry received many of its symbols from Africa rather than Africans receiving anything from freemasonry.

The work of Churchward was in the tradition of the researches of Gerald Massey, Leo Wiener, and other Europeans who looked to Africa for inspiration for their works. In his response to critics he maintained that all signs and symbols originated from the African's stellar, lunar, and solar mythos. Indeed, the original Australians were part of the African exodus. Churchward argues that the Egyptian *Book of the Dead* is the key to the door and without it one cannot "trace back the history of this world—the history of all religions, and the history of all mankind, and that which is attached thereto." Furthermore, Churchward says that:

> ... the first or Paleolithic man was the Pygmy, who was evolved in Central Africa at the sources of the Nile, or Nile valley, and that from here all originated and were carried throughout the world, and that the most primitive phase of mythology is a mode of representing certain elemental powers by means of living types which were superhuman, like the natural phenomena. The foundations of mythology were laid in the pre-anthropomorphic shape of primitive representation. Thus the typical giant, Apap, was an enormous water reptile. The typical *genetrix* and mother of life was a Water Cow that represented the earth; the typical provider was a goose, etc. It was here, in the Nile valley, that the dumb mythology became articulate. Egypt alone preserved primitive gnosis and gave expression to the language of signs and symbols, and it was here that the first elemental powers were divinized, here that Totemism, Stellar, Lunar and Solar Mythology originated. We say that the human race originated, or was planted, in the northeast of Africa (including the sources and the banks of the Nile), and it is a very important fact to note here that the symbology has been carried down amongst ourselves to the present day.[1]

We know that the city name *Athenai* and the divine name *Athene* or *Athena* derive from the Egyptian words *Ht Nt*. In antiquity, Athena was consistently identified with the Egyptian goddess *Nt* or *Neit*. They were virgin divinities of wisdom, weaving, and war. The cult of *Neit* was found around the city of Sais in the Western Delta. Sais was a secular name, the city's religious name was *Ht Nt* (Temple of House of Neit). The toponymic element *Ht-* is transcribed as *At-* or *Ath-*. It was also extremely common for Egyptian words to have what are called prothetic vowels before the first consonant. In this case the likelihood that *Nt* was preceded by a vowel is increased by the name *Anat*, given to a very similar West Semitic goddess. Some authorities believe that it is legitimate, correct, and proper to propose a vocalization of *At(h)anait* for *Ht Nt*. Also the lack of "i" in *Athene, Athana* in the Doric language and *A-ta-na* in Linear B is not a problem because both Doric and Attic use the variants *Athenaia* and *Athanaia*. The word in the times of Homer appears to be *Athenaie*. In fact, the semantic and philosophical arguments are equally as powerful as the phonetic one. Neith and Athena were two names for the same deity. Since in Egypt it was popular for a divinity to be addressed by the name of her or his dwelling it explains why some Greeks may have confused the names of the goddess and her city. Actually, it is reported that Charax of Pergamon in the second century A.D., said "the Saitians called their city Athenai."[2] This they could only say because to them Ht Nt was the name for Sais.

A method of historical or cultural analysis centered on African data must deal with the relationship of Africa to Europe generally and in antiquity Egypt to Greece particularly. The reason this is important is to establish for Africans in the Americas and in Africa the organic nature of the contribution of the Black world to the civilizing of Europe. Bernal says in *Black Athena*,

> "Sais was on the frontier of Egypt and Libya and was sometimes part Libyan, which explains Herodotos' detailed description of Athena's association with Libya; it is also clear that this first great Greek historian thought the Egyptians and some Libyans were black."[3]

If evidence suggests that Africa was the mother of European civilization, what force brought about the demise of respect for Africa? Greece gained in prominence while Egypt fell in reputation due to a combination of European racism and chauvinism. Africa's antiquity was no longer considered a valuable credit but rather a debit. Some writers have shown that the intensity of northern European racism was different and new. In fact, before the sixteenth century whites often celebrated dark skin. Racism grew with the European "voyages of discovery" where adventurers came into contact with diverse peoples. But it had existed in the early writings of Aristotle who saw the Greeks as superior to other people, particularly those who lived in cold regions of Europe and who, he believed, had courage but no brainpower and Asiatics who he said had brains but no courage. Racial superiority existed in Aristotle as it was to later exist in John Locke, David Hume, Voltaire, and Thomas Jefferson. In fact, as Bernal has shown, David Hume and Benjamin Franklin linked dark skin to moral and mental inferiority.

Chief among the views that increased the decline of Egypt in the minds of Europeans was the idea of polygenesis and geographic determinism. Both concepts are parts of the same cultural approach to race. Jean Bodin, Montesquieu and Rousseau all participated, from the French side, in this establishment of European superiority based on geography and topography. Of course, Aristotle placed Greece in the favorite position. Montesquieu's racism fully blossomed in his *Spirit of Laws* published in 1748 while Rousseau's *Social Contract* published in 1762 argued that Europe was the best repository of human achievement. Bernal has argued that the idea of progress and romanticism also assisted in the supplanting of Egypt and the rise of Greece. There is a clear changeover in the thinking of the Europeans from the fourteenth and fifteenth centuries. The impact of the translation into Italian of *Hieroglyphika,* a fifth century work by Horapollo, an Egyptian, was felt throughout Europe. This was almost the culmination of the early appreciation of Egypt by Europe.

By the beginning of the fifteenth century, Italian scholars had a good idea of the centrality of Egypt and the Hermetic Texts to the ancient learning they wished to revive. Scholars had long known about and read *Asclepius,* and Arabic Hermetic Texts were being translated into Latin. Furthermore, with the increase in contact between Italy and Greece the Neo-Platonic and Hermetic writings of Psellos and the other promoters of the Byzantine Renaissance became available.[4]

Our method, to be exact, must reconstruct the place of ancient Egypt in order to adequately deal with the history of Africa. In fact, the Europeans, particularly the Italians during the so-called Renaissance (it was a re-birth because of the primacy of Egypt) adopted Egyptian knowledge as the basis of their own. Actually the European Renaissance had a marked preference for information from ancient Egypt although some later defined it essentially as a Latin and Greece rebirth. It was the place where humans first dealt with the mysteries and with the possible exception of the Persians Zoroastrians and the ancient Indians and Chinese, the Egyptians in Africa were considered the source of all wisdom, art, and science. Of course, we know that Kemet and Nubia preceded the Greeks and the Romans. The Greeks and Romans attributed to the ancient Africans the *fontes* or sources of human wisdom.

Logos, Pathos, and Ethos were the pillars of proof the Greeks inherited from Africa. These pillars held the structures of the European Renaissance in many disciplines, but especially in philosophy, rhetoric, and ethics. Priestly training in Kemet had emphasized skills in rational explanation, the proper use of emotions and the character of the priest. A person who combined these traits could prove to be a wise priest. Aristotle who first wrote these proofs in Greek said that logos referred to logical appeals, pathos to emotional appeals, and ethos to character appeals. In Kemet, Imhotep is the most representative figure of this movement, although Pepi II must be considered significant.

The renunciation of these "pagan" ideas of proof and the institutionalization of Western notions of proof during the European Middle Ages constituted a major development in authoritative discussion. The influence of the barbarians was widespread. Entry of the Germanic tribes, Visigoths, Ostrogoths, and Vandals into the remnants of the Roman Empire and the Holy Roman Empire pressured the existing Christian pedagogical system inherited from the pagan Romans to adopt new concepts of proof. The Holy Roman Church, eager to extend its influence, bent to the demands of its new adherents who brought with them an extensive system of proof derived from their history. The Germans introduced oaths, ordeals and duels as the triune divinities of proof and in the process dethroned the pre-Christian ideas logos, pathos, and ethos. The Church acquiesced and permitted priests to serve as mediators, judges and officials in matters of proof. With the institutionalization of this trinity a person who was accused of a crime had the burden of proving himself innocent by one of the legitimate proofs: oath, ordeal or duel. No longer was it sufficient for a person to use mere logic, emotion, and character in a defense, he must demonstrate his innocence by successfully going through the trials. This concept of proof so enthusiastically adopted by the church was an attempt to delimit and conquer the pagan German gods by allowing the Christian God to assume the burden of protecting the innocent. Thus when one chose to prove his innocence what he was saying in effect was that God would allow him to pass the trial because a good God could not punish an innocent person. Many innocent persons lost their lives in a show of their righteousness.

Oaths required witnesses to the degree of the crime's severity and the accused social status. All accused persons could choose compurgators to bear witness to their oath-taking. If the accused should stumble or slip or forget the words of the oath, he was judged guilty. An innocent person would speak the words of the oath flawlessly. Ordeals were physical tests involving only the accused and usually were tests in extreme hot or cold. A person would be required to retrieve a pebble from a container of boiling water. If the hand manifested any type of burn the accused was adjudged guilty as charged. Sometimes the ordeal would require the accused to be tied with a rope and dropped in a body of water. If he sank, he was innocent; on the other hand, floaters were truly guilty because the nature of water, being purified by the priest and thereby holy, refused to receive a guilty, and therefore evil body into itself. How many innocent persons who were tried by this proof lived to celebrate their innocence is hard to say. Duels required the accused and the accuser to engage in a physical contest

against each other. Again the idea was the inevitability of innocence being protected by God.

When Pope Innocent called the Fourth Lateran Council in
1215 he explicitly forbade priests to officiate at ordeals and duels.
Proof of guilt or innocence was to be discovered in the proper
application of the scriptures. Only the priests in England obeyed,
probably at the behest of King John who owed Innocent a favor
for his declaration annulling the Magna Carta. Three years later,
however, when both John and Innocent were dead, the English
barons reinstated the Magna Carta. Throughout the Holy Roman
Empire the decline in Western European influences was felt as the
church imposed Christian culture with its Hebraic-Greco-Roman
ethos over the whole of Europe. Nevertheless, by this time the impact of the flirtation with competitive and combative proofs had
left an indelible imprint on Western notions of legitimacy.

The second historical development that assisted the sustenance
of legitimacy of institutions was the publication of Bishop Richard Whatley's *Elements of Logic* and *Essentials of Rhetoric,* 1826
and 1828 respectively. Whatley spent a lifetime defending Christian evidences. From his belief that the proof of God needed no
demonstration but that the disproof of God's existence needed
demonstration, he evolved the doctrines of *presumption* and *burden of proof.* Perhaps no two notions have aided and abetted the
maintenance of the status quo and the sustenance of institutional
legitimacy than presumption and burden of proof.

Presumption is the preoccupation of the ground. Something is presumed to be true unless arguments are adduced against it. *The burden of proof rests with the person who would move the presumption.* Changing the presumption from existing institutions has become increasingly more difficult as institutions have acquired new techniques for managing public impressions. Rather than operate as mere institutions pre-occupying ground and thus establishing their legitimacy and presumption, the institutions have gone on the offensive with the best traditions of oaths, ordeals, and duels. The pre-occupying institutions present their forms as the best possible institutions to do what they do and that there are no reasonable alternatives to be chosen. Defiance of the public coupled with invitation to challenge has become a common occurrence as institutions of power, whether academic or political, rest on their acquired positions.

A proper attitude toward human discovery and human knowledge depends on views that do not cast aside others' ways of knowing as unimportant. Indeed, any appropriate history cannot see some as in history and others as out of history. In this regard culture becomes more significant than civilizations as basis for moving toward universal respect and appreciation. For the Africologist, method must always possess Afrocentric place but not exclusive territory on phenomena. I speak of this type of method as a motive of Africological research, the soul of method.

It is necessary to examine what is meant by the soul of method.

I shall deal here with the meaning of soul as a concrete motive, in the sense of activator, in Afrocentric research. Soul is the vitality the researcher brings to the Afrocentric method, that is, the creative energy used to insure a successful project. The concept is similar to Wade Nobles' idea of cultural substance in the *Sakhu* that he sees as the "ontological principle of consubstantiation."[5] But I mean something more than an ontological principle when I say *soul of method*. This is not a mere oxymoron but what the Yoruba often call *asé, axé*, the force itself. Perhaps the only appropriate analogy to this concept of the soul of method is the vital genesis of form in African art where every art object acquires power as soon as it is consecrated in a particular way. Comments by a number of scholars underscore my observation in this regard. Horton has written of the Kalabari people that "it is men who make the gods important," and further "the forehead of the spirit ... implies not just something which is intimately linked to a spirit, but something which exercises a kind of control over it.'" Similarly, as *asé* exercises control over objects, soul exercises a guiding light over method. The indwelling vital energy must be present in the scholar's work for it to be successful. There is nothing mysterious in this type of appreciation of the human process of activating Afrocentric research. Indeed, the human personality keeps the *asé, axé,* active and vital. In research, the scholar must understand that everything is potentially active, powerful, and possible and it is up to the scholar to access the vitality of a project. This is different from any transmutation of matter into spirit as the European artist might reluctantly concede but rather spirit resides in matter by virtue of the universality of vital forces in objects. Thus, the soul of method responds not to clench forms for the benefit of some judgmental audience but to matter as represented in the carrying out of the method. In a fundamental way this approach differs from the European emphasis on prediction and individuality. Denis Williams observed several years ago in regards to artistic practice how African systems differed from European systems of art:

> "This difference between the two artistic systems, African and European, is reflected in the relative standpoints of the artist in the separate cultures. Where the practice of art for the European is individualistic and autobiographical, for the African it is anonymous and social."[6]

Williams recognizes in the field of art what the Africologists must understand when approaching a research project. Soul, as a concrete motive force, activates research by engaging the researcher in an effort to explain human functioning by relating to concrete human conditions and cultural factors. One has soul or uses soul effectively when one is able to transform strong emotional attachments to ideas to something that is external to one's self so that it is recognized, seen, and appreciated by others. One never dances alone and one certainly cannot have soul without the presence and appreciation of others.

African history and culture, as I have demonstrated, find their source and origin in the primacy of Africa in the development of human society. In addition, its zenith in antiquity was manifest in the Nile Valley Civilizations. There, the double-crown represented a union of regions, Upper and Lower Egypt, and the Per-aa was the lord of the two lands. Hence, almost from the beginning the history and the mythology of Africa were based on union. To wear the two crowns, the red and the white was to announce that conflict was symbolically overcome by joining the two parts. It is this history of acceptance, this adaptability; this ability to absorb without losing the essential character of expression that is the heart of the African method. Soul determines the character of the human project and establishes the possibility of an integrated approach to research. It qualifies as a principle of procedure, a protocol of action in that it makes it possible for a scholar to examine any phenomenon from many angles in a community. This eclecticism is welded into an integrated approach by soul, the emotional-intellectual evidence of a true union of the internal and the external.

The ancients understood that we were literally children of the earth, products of the organic system that is responsible for all we see. Humans were not of a different order from other materials of the earth. Since this was so it was clear to them that we were connected to everyone and everything. The fundamental mutability of cultures and civilizations never interferes with or contradicts the principle of human interconnectedness.

That soul represents a specific intervention in the method-ological process is a point that must be conceded on the basis of the historical and cultural evidence of African American scholarly inquiry. Of course, it is arguable that this event is not so much an intervention as the natural state of human method prior to cat-egorizing. In other words, the ancients who decided to gather ber-ries from certain bushes and to reject others were, in effect, par-ticipating in the same process by which we discover answers and solutions. Thus, the soul of method is structured but not structure in the sense of which the Structuralists speak.

Structuralism, even as a mode of thought, has taken on mean-ing in reference to the arrangement of parts such as in personality, architecture, and sentence structures. But the illusive Structural-ist's mode can be traced to Piaget's attempt to identify three struc-tural properties—wholeness, transformation, and self-regulation. In his explanation Piaget claims that a structure is a system of transformations that involve laws that preserve and enrich the structure itself.

The soul of method reveals itself in the formation of rhythm that is what I mean by a structure that is not the structure of the Structuralists. Kariamu Welsh expounds on the concept of rhythm as basic to the African aesthetic. Her conceptualization of this phenomenon relates directly to the idea of the soul of meth-od because what Piaget misses in his Structuralist formulation is the idea of rhythms. The concepts of wholeness, transformation, and self-regulation are without movement although Structuralism is considered the antithesis to formations built of aggregate elements. In this sense there is a false discourse bearing marks of betrayal of intellectual anticipation because to think of the constituents—wholeness, transformation, self-regulation—without rhythm is to see them as the very aggregation of elements that is anathema to the philosophical position of Structuralism itself. Part of the arguments raised against such a fixed, structured approach to reality arises through the concern the Afrocentrist has with the "force vital" within process. The concern is toward the direction of the truly organic, fluid, agreeable nature of rhythm, and the soul of method.

This becomes important when the scholar wishes to analyze the intricacies of the African American literary movements, or the nature of African American political power in urban centers, or the color issue among blacks in Brazil, or the European slave trade's disruption of the Guinea coast, or similar issues. Rhythm makes method responsive to a reality that is particularly efficacious if the scholar is able to tease out the insights that usually escape the mono-methodological perspective and Eurocentric approaches. One breaks the structured, lineal, monotony by investing research with soul, the rhythm of assessing and synthesizing in order to create understanding and meaning.

The acquisition of knowledge occurs within a social and political context defined by economic and historical factors. Thus, the individual scholar is engaged with the intersection of knowledge and the context. Not since Freud could a European scholar disclaim such an engagement. Indeed, Freud, if we must quote, wrote that the scholar must

> "...examine himself and *his own position in history,* the motives—perhaps hidden motives—which have guided his choice of theme or period and his selection and interpretation of the facts, "the *national and social background which has determined his angle of vision . . . ."*[7]

Ultimately what this means is that history is relative, that ethnography is biography, that definitions are personal because the scholar is engaged with the acquisition of knowledge in a social way. I agree, however, with Preiswerk and Perrot:

> "To state that history is relative, both to the personality of the historian and to the society from which he sprang, does not mean one adopts a stance, in the epistemology of history in favor of historicism and against other schools. It is first of all an epistemological position external to history, according to which *all* knowledge is the product of the action of a subject (in relation to a reality) and therefore is dependent on the cognitive behavior of this latter within a given social context."[8]

This raises the question of objectivity in research. Richards has pointed to the problems inherent in the concept that suggests that the scholar maintains a mental distance from the object of study. She shows that this is difficult to maintain and is at best an illusion. Why would a scholar want such a mental distance in the first place? Perhaps a more appropriate concept is *decentration* that is a process to reduce mental distance between subject and object of study. Although the Afrocentric method considers the separation of subject and object to be a transitory separation, the idea of a practical separation to allow engagement between scholar and subject is acceptable. In no case should a researcher deliberately falsify data for personal preferences. What becomes clear, however, in a study of numerous texts in the social sciences is that the Eurocentric writers have often written the prejudices of their societies into their texts. Many scholars have behaved toward African culture and history as pirates aboard a ship, they have taken as much as they could put under their belts and discarded the rest. The retrieval of African history remains the proper task of the Afrocentric scholars. Nothing could have demonstrated this any better than the CERTODOLA Conference in Yaounde, Cameroun in June, 2016 at the Mont Febe Hotel. Under the auspices of the *Centre International de Recherche et de Documentation sur les Traditions et les Langues Africaines* Charles Binam Benoi and Jean Biem brought some of the principal African thinkers together to hold a conversation on retrieving and preserving African cultural artefacts.

YAOUNDE AS THE CULMINATION OF DEBATE

The 2015 Yaounde meeting constituted the most serious gathering of African intellectuals in the Central African region in decades. Cameroun offered its template of various African cultures and political kingdoms as blessings for the powerful arguments for preservation made by a diverse group of African scholars including Ama Mazama from Guadeloupe and Molefi Kete Asante from the United States. Early interventions and questions set the tone for the debates about Afrocentricity and Eurocentricity that came to dominate some of the discussions. A guest professor opened the conference with a fairly good overview of the problems of African "development" that offered no way for Africans to escape from mental, political, and religious bondage. The indefatigable Jean Eudes Biem sought to raise the unspoken questions that he knew Asante and Mazama would ask of the participants. In fact, Mazama identified the principal problem with the preservation of African culture as the intellectual conquest of Africa by Europe and Arabia. Actually the minds of Africans, she contended, had imbibed too much of the philosophies, ideas, and values of others so that it would be impossible for them to achieve freedom from enslavement to Christianity or Islam. This was sensitive territory because neither the Christians nor the Muslims wanted to be questioned. Yet Biem was pleased that Mazama had raised the issues. He demonstrated good leadership but was trapped by the Eurocentrism of the chief African speaker on the main two days of the conference. Gregoire Biyogo of Gabon was given space to speak in Eurocentric terms about African Studies, affecting the some of the worst aspects of the European academy, he failed to see even after questioners put to him the Eurocentric bondage that he spewed forth as he demonstrated his reliance on only European scholarship. Some of the younger scholars were dismayed and did not relax until I took the floor to show him that Biyogo had erred in seeking to find Africa in the middle of Europe. Biyogo had some fascinating ideas about the Bamileke culture noting that *matta*, equity, might be related to the ancient Egyptian *maat* or *maa*, but he quoted only European scholars and basically ignored the works of Diop, Obenga, and Bilolo. This is neither good scholarship nor was it to be seen as proper given the purpose of the conference to speak of the preservation of African culture, history, philosophy, and languages. Once again we had highlighted our ability to master the colonial ideologies that were responsible for our condition. What we needed was a scholar who could do as Diop insisted connect Central Africa to the Nile Valley civilizations and tell the narrative as Africans should tell it.

DELANY AND BLYDEN: PIONEERS OF PROOF

During the mid-nineteenth century, two scholar-scientists appeared who would establish the intellectual bases of the Afrocentric reclamation of African history, both on the continent and in the Diaspora: Martin R. Delany and Edward Wilmot Blyden. Both of these men were considered by other Africans to be the very best the African people had produced in the Americas. Martin Robinson Delany, 1812-1885, was born in Charlestown, Vir-

ginia, now West Virginia There was perhaps no more contemporaneous African than Delany. Pride of birth and race made him
a veritable exception in his day. He knew that his heritage was
Kongo and Mandinka and that his grandfather had been a prince
when slave catchers caught him. Frederick Douglass speaking
on Delany's pride once remarked "I thank God for making me
a man simply; but Delany always thanks him for making him a
black man."

Delany's attitude was that there was no hope for the African
unless each African felt palpitating in his or her heart the entire
legacy of an historic people who abhorred slavery, prejudice, and
every archaic and Neanderthal idea about African inferiority.

Delany believed that in the subjugation of the African the
whites used elements of historical deceit; one based on the constant rumor that whites were naturally superior to blacks; the
other based on the corollary that blacks could not achieve in the
intellectual realm. He presented himself as a formidable challenge
to both arguments. In his person the deception was revealed and
as a scientist, ethnologist, explorer, and medical doctor, Delany
demonstrated the most exacting obligation to the idea of African centeredness.

Edward Wilmot Blyden, 1832-1912, attempted in a major way
to address the fundamental issues of Africans in contact with Europeans and Arabs. In effect, Blyden wanted to demonstrate that
the African, despite European propaganda, was not inferior to

Europeans but was the progenitor of human civilization. Blyden published *Christianity, Islam and the Negro Race*, in which he claimed that "the majority of American slave-holders are ... in justification of their most horrible system." Blyden could see little difference between the attitudes of the whites who had been slaveholders and the ones that had wished to be. They were both believers in the false idea of black racial inferiority.

Nevertheless, Blyden's philosophical outlook was optimistic and he saw himself as part of a vanguard in the African world seeking to reconnect African peoples to their origins and history.[9] A notion latent in Blyden's interpretation of history that later became a dominant motif in Diop is the necessity for the African to reconstruct his or her world, a world cruelly distorted by Europe. In Diop the spirit was more revolutionary as it captured the rhythmic movement of Africa's call for liberation. On the heels of Fanon's war drums for violent overthrow of the oppressors and the neocolonialists, Diop emphatically announced that the time had come for the African to center his/her historical experiences and to stop operating on the periphery of Europe. The power of Diop's insistence gathered to him numerous critics, chief of whom were continental Africans trained in European academies, particularly Ali Mazrui, Sulayman Nyang, and Isidore Okpewho. It was as if an African speaking from the standpoint of his own history and culture was somehow violating a fundamental principle of good scholarship. It was almost as if they did not want Diop to express himself from his own worldview or from within his own paradigm of learning and knowledge. Mazrui, like Diop, was a Muslim. He saw in Diop a rival for African Islamic intellectual hegemony. But Mazrui was no match for Diop in the breadth of his knowledge and the loyalty to African traditions as essential for African advancement. In fact, Diop was a Muslim by birth like many African Americans are Christians by birth; Diop was fundamentally African in his orientation. Neither Arab nor European realities moved him away from his insistence on the blackness of ancient Kemet.

The Unfortunate Cynic's Turn

Ali Mazrui, an eloquent speaker and poetic writer, emerges at his height as a rhetorician capable of handling language in an eloquent fashion but his rhetoric is misleading due to internal ambiguity and isolation from the discourse on method established by Afrocentrists. Indeed, his denial of this discourse has contributed to his ambiguity and the internal ambiguity results from his isolation from the general spirit of the African intellectual world; a world that is not devoted to Arab or European interests but one that is strictly trying to rescue African people from the mental slavocracy that has prevailed in the academies. This is not to say that his political insights have been useless because they have been quite stimulating in their wit. My concern with Mazrui is more profound than a discussion of his rhetoric although it is impossible to avoid it because he has given us some wonderful passages.

Mazrui's cynicism about Africa colors his entire corpus; he is at once alienated and conflicted in his assessment of the political and historical phenomena he finds on the continent. In many ways I see Mazrui as the spiritual father of the Ugandan writer Mahmoud Mamdani because like Mazrui the younger scholar, also Muslim, rarely highlights the indigenous culture of Africa. Mazrui is the source of this particular school of African thinking. This is not to say that he has not been perceptive but rather to point out that he has rarely advanced the idea of Africa. In effect, Mazrui becomes a truly Eurocentric Africanist of the genre that has been schooled in the discipline most advantageous to the advancement of a European intellectual particularism. What is valuable to note here is that African birth does not make one Afrocentric; Afrocentricity is a matter of intellectual discipline and must be learned and practiced. In Mazrui's case we see insight but not Afrocentric insight and one can certainly appreciate the quality of his wit and the manner of his style without acceding to him an Afrocentric perspective. Indeed, he is essentially an apologist for Arab penetration of Africa in cultural and political terms. Thus, the notion of the triple heritage of Africa as advanced in Mazrui's documentary *The Africans* and other of his works. This formula is, however, an oversimplification since both the European and Arab or Christian and Muslim heritages are for the most part of recent origin. Certainly the Coptic traditions of Egypt and the Ge'ez traditions of Ethiopia are Christian without European influences dating from the first century; the Islamic heritage dates from the Arab invasion of Egypt in the seventh century A.D. However, the history of Africa reaches many thousands of years back from the period of the Christian and Islamic influences. What one could say with some degree of accuracy is that Christianity and Islam have been grafted upon the African heritage. One does not speak of the triple heritage of Europe, for example, even though millions of Muslims live in Europe as well as millions of Christians. In fact, if we took the major religions that are practiced in a region of the world and assessed the heritage of the region on the basis of those religions we would find that most areas of the world have a multiplicity of "influences." Mazrui is incorrect, however, in granting to Christianity and Islam the same place as the traditional and centering African culture found throughout the continent, perhaps less so in some places because of the density and intensity of the oppression and suppression of the indigenous people.

In effect, Mazrui does not transcend his particular vision of Africa because of an ideological entrapment: combining both European and Arab hegemonic positions over the intellectual and cultural resources of Africa. Indeed, Mazrui sees in Africa's enforced accommodation to Christianity and Islam a reason to rejoice that Africa demonstrates the possibility of ecumenicalism. Were he able to see Africa from an Afrocentric perspective he would question the imposition of Arabic or European influences on Africa, especially where those influences have disrupted the cultural, artistic, economic, and political lives of African peoples.[10]

In his brilliant dissection of Mazrui's views, "The Fallacy of the `Triple Heritage' Thesis: A Critique," Habtu argues that Mazrui's line of inquiry was Eurocentric.[11] A more successful path to knowledge, he contends, might be to examine the African contribution and influence on Judaism, Arab, Western, Graeco-Roman and other ways of thinking.

Habtu says that Diop was perhaps the first to suggest this approach in unequivocal terms in his book *The African Origin of Civilization*. Habtu's critique is devastating for the Euro-Africanists and Arabo-Africanists led by Mazrui. He asserts that they speak of a Graeco-Roman or Judaeo-Christian heritage but do not choose to speak of Egypto-Hellenic, Egypto-Judaic, Nilo-Kongo or Nilo-Nguni-Sudanic heritage.[12] Of course, Mazrui is unable to think Afrocentrically and Habtu's criticism exposes Mazrui's inability to transcend the Africanist cocoon that views Africa as a receptor, a passive continent, incapable of influencing others and perhaps forever a beggar continent in term of ideas and concepts. There are reasons for Mazrui's difficulty with an Afrocentric perspective.

Mazrui's epigrammatic style, while often engaging, conceals the essentially liberal European orientation of his work. His critique of Africa is severed from any identifiable African school of thought. In fact, Mazrui assumes that he stands within no tradition in Africa but, of course, he is most traditional in his acceptance and practice of Eurocentric analysis of Africa. While this is properly not an African School of Thought it is framed in Africa and among Africans due to the heavy presence of European intellectual traditions on Africans.

Mazrui's ambiguity is directly related to his worldview. By conceiving of Africa as the receptor of others' views and ideologies he strips Africa of its productive and generative subjectivity. He sees the continent always as the acted-upon, victim, and powerless. His is an analysis of weakness where it is necessary to question the basis of strength. Mazrui's confusion is a liberal confusion found whenever the Afrocentrists call for the humanization of the world. Afrocentricity as the intellectual movement that restored the place of Africans in world history and reestablished the human project in centeredness remains fundamental to the Afrocentric revolution and place of Africa prior to Arab and European colonialism. Mazrui, for example, wants to start with Arab infiltration and to claim it as an equal legacy with the indigenous African contributions. Afrocentrists aim to see Africa as a part of the human equation in everything, to reject all attempts to take science, art, literature, music and theology out of Africa. Therefore, the work to humanize Africa, that is, to assist nature in transforming the environment for human fulfillment, is in the end not a plan to Africanize the world but to humanize it.

We cannot yet begin to speak of a post-Diopian world in a strict sensebecause this is the age of Diop without whom the dignity ofAfricans would have continued to be defended, as Du Bois admirably did, by appeals to Eurocentric frames of reference. Diop freedus from that dependence. He argued that the objectivity of knowledge referred to by European scholars could not be separated fromconsciousness of the social-cultural world and that Europeansbrought that consciousness with them whenever they discussedAfrica. This is why Hegel's knowledge of Africa is dimmed by hisparticipation in the European conception of Africa; this is why theAfrican, freed from the social-cultural consciousness imposed byEuropean education can see the brightness of his/her own history.African American scholars have been the principal proponentsof Diop's ideas, although on the continent and in Europe there have been scholars like Theophile Obenga, Mubabinge Bilolo, Martin Bernal, Fergus Sharman, Kimani Nehusi, and Lusala Nkuka, who haveadvanced various aspects of Diop's historiography.

THE CULTURAL CONTEXT FOR KNOWLEDGE ACQUISITION

I have said that acquisition of knowledge occurs in a cultural context. What, then, is culture? In the sense that the Afrocentrists speak of it culture refers to the learned and shared values, attitudes, predispositions, and behavior patterns of a human group that can be transmitted. Thus, I consider world voices, worldviews, cosmogonies, institutions, ideas, myths, epics, and symbols as comprising culture.

The preservation of knowledge depends upon retentive mechanisms such as human memory, computers, writing systems, video and audio recorders on one level and libraries, repositories, museums, and archives another level. Writing, however, has become a major avenue for retention and preservation. Ngugi has explained how writing ought to be viewed:

> "Writing is representation of sounds with visual symbols, from the simplest knot among shepherds to tell the number in a herd or the hieroglyphics among the Agikuyu Gicaandi singers and poets of Kenya, to the most complicated and different letter and picture writing systems of the world today."[13]

The valorization of European letters and the degradation of African letters, writing, communication systems and visions show, as in the case of the late Kamuzu Banda's setting up of a Malawian private school where Africans cannot teach, the most servile intellectual behavior on the part of Africans. Banda embodied by virtue of this example of self-hatred, the most violent form of anti-African ideas. He established the Kamuzu Academy to train young Malawians in English. But no Malawian was allowed to teach at Kamuzu when it opened in 1982. It was a grammar school designed to produce boys and girls who would be sent to universities like Harvard, Chicago, Oxford, Cambridge and Edinburgh. Banda falsely believed that only associating with Europeans could bring enlightenment and knowledge. He instructed that Latin should occupy a central place in the curriculum. All teachers must have had at least some Latin in their academic background. Dr. Banda said that no one could fully master English without knowledge of languages such as Latin and French. He had no faith in African languages. This is why the reaction of Dlamini-Zuma was so magnificent for the Pan African world when during the contest for the leadership of the African Union she responded to a suggestion that she was an Anglophone that her first language was Zulu and that she did not consider herself an Anglophone. Jean Ping, the out-going leader of AU, may have been a Francophone, but Dr. Nkosazana Dlamini-Zuma of South Africa made her choice clear.

From the European cultural center, Africa is usually seen as marginal, uncivilized and on the periphery of historical consciousness. Some of the statements of European writers reveal the extent of their attack on African intelligence. Examine the works of such geniuses of racism as a Rider Haggard or a Nicholas Monsarrat; not to mention the pronouncement of some of the giants of Western intellectual and political establishment, such as Hume ("... the negro is naturally inferior to the whites ... "), Thomas Jefferson ("... the blacks ... are inferior to the whites endowments of both body and mind ... "), or Hegel with his Africa comparable to a land of childhood still enveloped in the dark mantle of the night as far as the development of self-conscious history was concerned.

FOUNDATIONS OF AN APPROACH

The practical reasons for advancing an Afrocentric method are found in the manner Africa has been studied by Africanists as well as non-Africanists. Since the Eurocentric methods have been aggressive and violative, it is necessary to demonstrate a humanistic method capable of allowing for the acquisition of data from all societies, African, American, European, Asian, and Indigenous Peoples. This means that the method will have to deal with the questions of exploitation of data, transformation of data, theft of data, and distortion of data. Ngugi wa Thiong'o has maintained that the "cultural bomb" is more damaging to a people than the military and economic weapons.

He eloquently describes the impact of this intellectual and cultural war on Africa in these words:

"The effect of a cultural bomb is to annihilate a people's belief in their names, in their languages, in their environment, in their heritage of struggle, in their unity, and in their capacities and ultimately in themselves. It makes them see their past as one wasteland of non-achievement and it makes them want to distance themselves from that wasteland. It makes them want to identify with that which is furthest removed from themselves, for instance, with other peoples' languages rather than their own. It makes them identify with that which is decadent and reactionary, all those forces that would stop their own springs of life. It even plants serious doubts about the moral rightness of struggle. Possibilities of triumph or victory are seen as remote, ridiculous dreams. The intended results are despair, despondency and a collective deathwish. Amidst this wasteland which it has created, imperialism presents itself as the cure and demands that the dependent sing hymns of praise with the constant refrain: "Theft is holy." Indeed, this refrain sums up the new creed of the neocolonial bourgeoisie in many independent African states."[14]

Ngugi's "cultural bomb" was dropped on Africa long ago. Its ramifications have fallen-out over the entire scope of knowledge about the continent, poisoning the streams of inquiry as well as the fountains of truth. Chinweizu in *Decolonising the African Mind* concludes that Africans have seldom stood their ground to defend their customs, culture, or economies. According to Chinweizu both Europeans and Arabs have exploited the continent because Africans have not been able to establish a collective sense of responsibility.[15] Chinweizu believes that the cultural bombardments by Europe and Arabia have taken their toll on African will to overcome.

HERODOTUS AND AFRICA

Some European historians have quarreled with the writings of Herodotus and Diogenes in an attempt to undermine Africa's contributions to world civilization. Other scholars have introduced spurious concepts, that is, they have invented illusive concepts and tried to invest them with meaning to create confusion around African phenomena. Africologists study all branches of knowledge with the aim of throwing Afrocentric light on African phenomena. Therefore, it is proper to consider the works of Herodotus as pertinent to our understanding.[16]

Herodotus was the most comprehensive of the early Greek recorders of the customs, traditions, and civilizations of North Africa. In the fifth century B.C., Herodotus observed four distinct groups of people in the part of Africa where he travelled. Two groups were indigenous to Africa; the other two groups were foreign to the continent. The indigenous people Herodotus called Ethiopians and Libyans, probably ancestors to the Tubu and Khawerghans. The foreign people were Phoenicians and Greeks. The latter had been influenced by the customs of the Africans. Both the Libyans and Ethiopians (Herodotus considered the Egyptians to be a branch of the Ethiopian people) spoke a similar Hamitic language. As John Jackson says, "Anyone who speaks a Hamitic language is a Hamite, and there is no necessary racial connotation involved. But certainly the idea once widely entertained, that the ancient Hamites of Africa were of Caucasoid origin is demonstrably untenable."[17] Indeed Harry Johnston, who is cited widely on the Hamites defined them as "That Negroid race which was the main stock of the ancient Egyptian, and is represented at the present day by the Somali, the Galla and some of the blood of Abyssinia and of Nubia, and perhaps by the peoples of the Sahara Desert."[18]

As the late Martin Bernal has shown in *Black Athena,* Herodotus considered Africa as the land of black people. Indeed, Herodotus' account of an expedition of young African men from the Nasamonian region who travelled across the Sahara to the Niger River is most explicit:

"They said there had grown up among them some wild young men, the sons of certain chiefs, when they came to man's estate, indulged in all manner of extravagances, and among other things drew lots for five of their number to go and explore the desert parts of Libya, and try if they could not penetrate further than any had done previously....The young men therefore, dispatched, on this errand by their comrades with a plentiful supply of water and provisions, travelled at first through the inhabited region, passing which they came to the wild beast tract, whence they finally entered upon the desert, which they proceeded to cross in a direction from east to west. After journeying for many days over a wide extent of sand, they came at last to a plain where they observed trees growing; approaching them, and seeing fruit on them, they proceeded to gather it. While they were thus engaged, there came upon them some dwarfish men, under the middle height, who seized them and carried them off. The Nasamonians could not understand a word of the language, nor had they any acquaintance with the language of the Nasamonians. They were led across extensive marshes and finally came to a town, where all the men were of the height of their conductors, and black complexioned. A great river flowed by the town, running from west to east and containing crocodiles."[19]

Furthermore, Martin Bernal leaving the ancient Egyptians and Libyans that he knows as black people claims that Northern Africa was the home of black people long after the period of the Nasamonians. He states that "The Numidian and Mauritanian kings and chiefs allied themselves to the Romans because they desired home rule of self-government, and for that reason they wanted the power of Carthage destroyed, as Carthaginian influence was already making itself felt in their internal and external affairs. But no sooner had the Numidian kings and chiefs assisted Rome to destroy Carthage than Rome picked a quarrel with them and annexed their country. The Mauritanian kings, who occupied part of modern Morocco and Algeria, had hoped to exercise self-determination and enjoy full self-government, but this was not to be. Within the hundred-odd years from the fall of Carthage in 146 B.C. to 42 B.C., Rome incorporated or absorbed into her Empire the regions equivalent to western Tripolitania, Tunisia, and all the coastal regions of Algeria and Morocco. Rome also annexed the old Greek colonies in Cyrenaica, and in 30 B.C. added the newly acquired territory of Egypt to the Cyrenaican possessions in order to form a Roman province."[20]

Unfortunately unlike Bernal, Edward Said earlier writes in *Orientalism* about these issues in terms of European versus Orient social and cultural worlds and consequently follows in Europe's footsteps by misunderstanding Africa and misplacing a part of Africa in the Orient. In fact, Said writes that:

"There is very little consent to be found, for example, in the fact that Flaubert's encounter with an Egyptian courtesan produced a widely influential model of the Oriental woman; she never spoke of herself, she never represented her emotions, presence, or history. He spoke for and represented her. He was foreign, comparatively wealthy, male, and these were historical facts of domination that allowed him not only to possess Kuchuk Hanem physically, but to speak for her and tell his readers in what way she was "typically Oriental." My argument is that Flaubert's situation of strength in relation to Kuchuk Hanem was not an isolated instance. It fairly stands for the pattern of relative strength between East and West, and the discourse about the Orient that it enabled."[21]

But when he writes thusly he is speaking about Arabs in Egypt, an African country with a history steeped in the traditions of African people. Flaubert's woman could not have been an authentically African woman and that is why Said is able to make his trope work for the reader. In other words, Said claims Egypt for the Orient in much the same way the French had done in the Eighteenth Century after Napoleon's invasion. To further tie Africa to the Orient, Said uses Egypt in conjunction with India, not in conjunction with Sudan or Chad, but India in Asia that could properly be referred to as a part of the Orient. In fact, Said writes:

> "I doubt that it is controversial, for example, to say that an Englishman in India or Egypt in the later nineteenth century took an interest in those countries that was never far from their status in his mind as British colonies. To say this may seem quite different from saying that all academic knowledge about India and Egypt is somehow tinged and impressed with, violated by, the gross political fact—and yet *that is what I am saying* in this study of Orientalism."[22]

What is perhaps most peculiar is Said's submission to the attempt to connect Sanskrit and the Indo-Aryan language project in such a way as to take Egypt out of Africa. In other words, the classical African civilizations of the Nile Valley came to be seen in a conceptual way, in Said's thinking, as attached to India and Sanskrit studies, further divorcing Egypt from Africa. Said says

> "Yet at certain moments of that general European history of interest in the East, particular parts of the Orient like Egypt, Syria, and Arabia cannot be discussed without also studying Europe's involvement in the more distant parts, of which Persia and India are the most important; a notable case in point is the connection between Egypt and India so far as eighteenth- and nineteenth-

century Britain was concerned. Similarly, the French role in deciphering the Zend-Avesta, the preeminence of Paris as a center of Sanskrit studies during the first decade of the nineteenth century, the fact that Napoleon's interest in the Orient was contingent upon his sense of the British role in India: all these Far Eastern interests directly influenced French interest in the Near East, Islam, and the Arabs."[23]

For all his clarity in exposing the European prosecution of a false discourse on Orientalism, Said is terribly confused on the issue of Egypt and can be credited with making some awful declarations about Egypt. Distinction must be made between Ancient Egypt and Arabic Egypt. Ancient Egypt is a black civilization. Arabic Egypt is a cultural hegemony on the indigenous population that began in 639 CE. However, the preceding passage demonstrates an attempt to totally dismiss the presence of Africans. In order to write such a passage Said has to buy into the very same discourse he endeavors to overthrow. But since his aim is to vindicate the Arabs against the Europeans he leaves Africans invisible in the process. This does not work except as a further obfuscation of the Kemetic reality. Said could have profited from reading the works of Diop whom he obviously did not know. Nevertheless, he mentions the inclination of H. A. R. Gibbs, an eminent student of Arabic, to call himself an Orientalist instead of an Arabist when in fact he was most particularly an Arabist. But Said is particularly incorrect regarding the place of Sanskrit when he adds to the mythology of the preeminence of Sanskrit as a language. The question is preeminent to what? Research has long since demonstrated the anteriority of ancient *kiKam* or *ciKam* to other African languages and its primacy as a civilizing language in Northeast Africa and Southwest Asia. Despite this fact Edward Said is content to write:

> "When around the turn of the eighteenth century the Orient definitively revealed the age of its languages—thus outdating Hebrew's divine pedigree—it was a group of Europeans who made the discovery, passed it on to other scholars, and preserved the discovery in the new science of Indo-European philology."[24]

A proper critique would have demonstrated that the Indo-European philological school did not possess the antiquity of the ancient African Pharaonic language and that the so-called Orient language was African. In fact, numerous scholars have now shown that *ciKam*, the language of Kemet, ancient Egypt, has its source in the *kiSwahili*-Bantu languages of southern Africa. One would have thought that Said would have interrogated more deeply the source of African languages since he knew that science had concluded that the origin of the human race was Africa. The best we can get out of Said is that:

> "As early as 1804 Benjamin Constant noted in his *Journal Intime* that he was not about to discuss India in his *De la religion* because the English who owned the place and the Germans who studied it indefatigably had made India the *fons et origo* of everything; and then there were the French who had decided after Napoleon and Champollion that everything originated in Egypt."[25]

The truth of the matter is that Egypt predates Indian civilization and language by several thousands of years. More significantly the great voice of Buddha is only present in the 6th century BC and by that time the Egyptian civilization had gone through four Golden Periods, including the *Age of the Pyramids*, the *Restoration of the Mentuhoteps*, the *18th and 19th Dynasties*, and the *Nubian Restoration*. These periods are before Buddha, Jesus, and Mohammed and suggest that Africans did not wait until they heard from the Greeks, Romans, or Arabs to build the greatest monumental civilization the world had ever known.

Although some consider the commencement of "Orientalism" to be found in the decision of the Church Council of Vienna in 1312 to establish chairs in Arabic, Greek, Hebrew, and Syriac at the universities in Paris, Oxford, Bologna, Avignon and Salamanca the real period of the movement to take Egypt out of Africa and place it in the Orient was the nineteenth century when Princeton, Chicago, Pennsylvania, London, Paris and Berlin founded schools of Oriental studies.

Quite frankly, the only reason Egypt is considered by Edward Said as a part of the Orient is the Arabic language, a language not indigenous to Africa, although many words thought to be Arabic are actually African words according to Fergus Sharman. Arabic, Turkish, and Persian (Farsi) were studied by d'Herbelot, Galland, and Hottinger, either separately or as a group, in what was to be called Oriental studies. Although Arabic was spoken in Egypt, it was not the original or ancient Egyptian language; the locus of the language is Arabia.

It should be noted, however, that Napoleon developed an Institut d'Egypte soon after the 1799 invasion. This institute was soon to be overshadowed by the various schools of Oriental studies. As European knowledge of Africa increased, its hostility toward the classical civilizations of the Nile became more complex.

Nowhere has the pantheon of distinguished icons of cultural faith been more rewarding for seekers than ancient Africa. In classical Africa one finds the world of the Sphinx, Auset, Ausar, Heru, Kagemni, Kety, Nefertari, Hatshepsut, Rameses, Prester John, Imhotep, Tutankhamen, Seti, Piankhy, and Tarharka. No region on earth was any richer for the seeker after ancient truths.

Napoleon's aim in Africa was to subdue Egypt and thereby gain access to the glory of classical Africa. A byproduct was to be the outmaneuvering of Britain. With the Treaty of Campo Formio behind him, in 1797 while in Italy Napoleon plotted the overthrow of Egypt. Fascinated in his youth by Egypt and particularly the conquest by Alexander of the country in the fourth century B.C., Napoleon saw himself as the new Alexander reconquering the most ancient part of Africa. The fact that Egypt's culture had become essentially a new Islamic outpost further intrigued him since he could begin to repay the Muslims for their long occupation of Spain, Sicily and portions of France. He relied upon French scholars to assess the difficulty of taking Egypt.

Napoleon's enlistment of several dozen "savants" for his Egyptian Expedition is too well known to require detail here. His idea was to build a sort of living archive for the expedition, in the form of studies conducted on all topics by the members of the Institut d'Egypte, which he founded. What is perhaps less well known is Napoleon's prior reliance upon the work of the Comte de Volney, a French traveler whose *Voyage en Egypte et en Syrie* appeared in two volumes in 1787.

Napoleon refers to Volney in his own memoirs *Campagnes d'Egypte et de Syrie, 1798-1799* which were dictated while he was held at Saint Helena. He used every device to gain the advantage for the Armee d'Egypte, even to the extent of telling the Muslims of Egypt that the French Army soldiers were the true Muslims. Convinced that a demonstration of piety would win over the Muslims, Napoleon made a proclamation in Alexandria on July 2, 1798, in order to show that he was in support of Islam! Later just to emphasize his belief in Islam, Napoleon tried to underscore his scheme by convincing the Muslim teachers of his sincerity. Like Alexander hundreds of years before declaring that he was the "son of God," Napoleon relied on the religious fervor of his hosts to gain advantage. To this end, the sixty *ulemas* who taught at the Al-Azhar were invited to his quarters, given full military honors, and then were flattered by Napoleon's admiration for Islam and Mohammed and by his obvious veneration for the Koran, with which he seemed perfectly familiar. This worked, and soon the population of Cairo seemed to have lost its distrust of the occupiers.

The most daring part of Napoleon's occupation was the thoroughness with which he intended to conquer the culture of Egypt. No conqueror prior to him had been so ruthless in his scheme to gain dominance over the legacy of the ancients. Indeed, after the Roman Empire, the Byzantine Empire, the Arabs, and the Mamelukes had all occupied Egypt? Although the Arabs had been in Egypt the longest and their influence on the culture was most telling their occupation never possessed the aggressive character of Napoleon's adventure. While the Arabs neglected African history by occupying the land with little interest in the history, the Armee d'Egypte occupied the history of Egypt and sought to record, study, dissect, and appropriate the whole of the civilization. In the massive work, *Description de l'Egypte,* published between 1809 and 1828 in twenty-three volumes, the French attempted to demonstrate their total acquisition of Egypt intellectually.

DEVIATION AND CONFUSION

The continental African "Africanist" Sulayman Niang has made some incredible comments about the role of Islam in Africa. As I have said regarding Mazrui earlier it appears that the aim of some scholars is to bring Africa without clothes into the arena of humanity. Nyang's analysis leaps toward an Afrocentric account of that interaction. However, he is trapped by his own identification with Islam and consequently misconstrues the nature of the

Abrahamic tradition's intrusion into Africa. In his method Nyang
also insists on claiming for Islam something that he never claims
for African intelligence: creativity and consciousness. He fails to
grasp the impact of intrusions on African culture. Nyang believes
that in some respects this invasion may be valuable to Africa.

> "In my view, the African encounter with the Abrahamic tradition
> has been very inspiring and spiritually elevating. The message of
> Abraham, as echoed and preached by the Old Testament proph-
> ets, Christ and Muhammad, is still reverberating in the African
> spiritual firmaments. The ringing of church bells and the boom-
> ing voices of latter-day Bilal's summoning fellow believers to
> prayer, make it crystal clear to all observers that Africa has finally
> joined the growing commonwealth of believers in the Abraha-
> mic tradition. The African decision to embrace the Abrahamic
> tradition is significant in many respects. To put it another way, I
> would say that the African encounter with the Abrahamic tradi-
> tion is going to be, in the long run, beneficial to the Africans as
> well as their fellow worshippers elsewhere on the planet. Africa's
> gift to the followers of the Abrahamic tradition will be the spirit
> of cultural tolerance in a world of ethnic diversity."[26]

However, there is no triple heritage of Africa; there is the double legacy of Islam and Christianity impacting on the indigenous
culture of the continent emerging as "double trouble" for African
expression. Nyang goes so far as to say, "In my view, the key concept
in traditional African thought is the cosmic schizophrenic tendencies of man."[27] Nyang explains that this means the world of concrete
reality, the world of social values, and the world of inexpressible
spiritual powers. While there is a basis for Nyang's philosophical

divisions in the ethical system of Africa there is no justification for calling these divisions "cosmic schizophrenic tendencies" as if they reflect a psychological disorder. Such discourse about traditional African society betrays Nyang's difficulty in resolving his own dilemma. For example, he calls African emphasis on social values and the traditions of the ancestors an "overemphasis." Or take his conclusion that Arabic succeeded in becoming the language of the north of Africa because of "its prestige and usefulness."[28] That statement overlooks the truth because it is more correct to say that the language succeeded because of force and punishment. No language is more useful than any other and all languages have the same capacity depending upon the challenges that are called upon by circumstances. How would Africans see Arabic as prestigious? This borders on racist thinking and it should have never entered the discourse on African identity. If the Ukrainians spoke Russian at one time it was because of the domination of Russian culture; if black people in Nigeria speak English it is because of colonial domination. So it is with the pervasiveness of Arabic in North Africa; it is a reflection of power as expressed in conquest and oppression.

Once more an African scholar whose ancient ancestors were the first to name god allows his recent religion to cloud his judgment about African history. Of course, Nyang knows he is in trouble when he writes:

"In fact, in talking about the Islamic contribution to the social universe of the African, one could argue that the arrival of Islam in the continent widened the horizons of the traditional African a little bit. Whereas in the past this man had entrusted destiny to the hands of the spirits who resided in a well, a tree or a stream somewhere in the ecological setting of his tribal group, whereas he wished to placate the gods and ancestors, under the Islamic religion he found that his life was for appointed time and that his deeds on earth did have singular meaning."[29]

Nyang is, of course, carried away with the valorization of Islam. He writes:

"Another area where the early Muslims could have affected the minds and hearts of the traditional Africans was their possession of the powers of the written word. This technology of intellectual conservation must have deeply impressed their early African hosts in the West Sudan, for it must have looked like a miracle to them that a man could reduce long court proceedings into signs and symbols."[30]

Any Afrocentric method would begin with the consciousness of the African populations rather than the "imposed" consciousness of the Muslims. No assessment has been made of the values, beliefs, and attributes of the culture of Africans before Nyang tells us that the Africans must have thought the reduction of court proceedings to signs and symbols was miraculous.[31] Obviously the writer neither understands nor appreciates the diversity and complexity of African graphic systems.

Furthermore, I cannot see why the Muslim missionaries should not have thought it "miraculous" that the African judges could sit for three days listening to arguments of adversaries and then present those arguments verbatim to the satisfaction of the principals. What Nyang has done here is to take the Eurocentric valorization of the alphabet as his leading concept. For Nyang, the African is the only one "reduced" to wonderment.[32] This was not true then and it certainly is not true now. The Afrocentrist, basing analysis on concrete human behaviors, discovers interactive wonderment on the parts of all parties. Without such a view, the scholar simply assumes ideas, concepts and terms imposed by Arab or European writers to be a priori correct. One sees the danger of this blind allegiance to "concepts" in the use of the word "negro," for example.

THE USE OF THE TERM "NEGRO"

There is no ethnic group in Africa that calls itself *negro* or its language *negro*. The term is preeminently a creation of the European mind to refer to any African group or people who correspond to a certain negative image of culture. The term is meaningless in reality but has become a useful word for those who would serve a political purpose by the term. Thus, the word *negro* is used by white writers to obfuscate as in the following examples: "Some such movements are probably reflected in the ever recurrent tradition that the early dynasties of Egypt were of Ethiopian origin. It is perhaps too often assumed that Ethiopian is necessarily the equivalent of *negro*." Here, for example, in a book published in 1967, MacMichael is debating with history. He uses the term "negro" as it is an inferior people. Ethiopians (Shoa, Amhara, Galla, etc.) are one branch of the African people as Egyptians and Zulu and Yoruba are branches of the African people. "Negro" on the other hand is introduced to obscure the Africanity of the Classical Per-aa civilizations.

The European writers often translated the ancient texts in the light of their contemporary political realities. No ancient African text mentions the word "negro." It simply does not exist, but the European writers took liberty to empower certain expressions in the texts with their own social conventions. Consider MacMichael's discussion of the origin of the ethnic name Nuba.

> "This term first occurs in literature in the geography of Eratosthenes, who was born in 287 B.C. He speaks of the Nuba. Later the name occurs as Nubato, or in the Latinized form of Nobatae." [33]

The ultimate derivation of the word is not known, but it appears to be of very ancient origin and may be connected through the Coptic word *Noybt* (meaning "to plait") with *"nebved,"* the word used in the inscription of Thutmoses I (date c. 1540 B.C.) to denote "the plaited-haired ones" whom that Per-aa overthrew in the neighborhood of the third cataract. It can best be translated as: "He has overthrown the King of the Nubians (Nehesi); the Nubian is helpless.... There is not a remnant left among the plaited-haired ones who came to attack him." [34] MacMichael had used the word *Negro* in his text but the best translation of Nehesi remains as it was Nubian; it is a nationality not a race. MacMichael's rendering is typical of the Eurocentric use of terms that have no meaning for Africans. Perhaps the best example of MacMichael's racist subtleties is revealed in the following statement:

> "It may be the case, and probably is, that the southern Nuba are to some extent the modern representatives of the race of Negroes who temporarily held Dongola and the cataract country south of Halfa in the days of the Middle Kingdom and early Empire and whose congeners, no doubt at a later date, formed part of the forces of the Ethiopian dynasty that conquered Egypt and ruled it for something less than a century, but these negroes were aliens in the northern Sudan and most of them were forced back to the south, and their place in Lower Nubia was taken by its original inhabitants and settlers from Egypt."[35]

The writer has and gives no evidence for the preceding statement. It is purely based on the social realities of the writer. Again the use of "negroes" obfuscates the African reality. Furthermore, the "race of negroes" he speaks of are Africans, as are the Nuba of whom he is writing. The statement that "these negroes were aliens" is incredible inasmuch as the people of the Sudan were Africans and without giving an ethnic name one cannot say whether these people were aliens or not. There is no *negro* ethnic group or race. The intellectual confusion that reigns in the use of racial classifications by white scholars who apply contemporary social conventions is seen in statements like the following:

> "The Middle Nubian stock was also mixed, it is probable, with another strain, that of the red-skinned Beja from the eastern deserts. But in the main, from Assuan for some distance south of Halfa, it was negroid, though certainly not true negro."[36]

Do these "negroes" have culture, language, or civilization? Are they without a name other than the modern European creation *negro* or true Negro?

MacMichael is unrepentant, he reaches back to Kashta, the African king who had his capital at Gebel Barkal (Napata) in 750 B.C. and claims, with no evidence given, that Kashta, one of the great leaders of Africa invaded Egypt and established his supremacy as far as Waset and had under his control "subjects who were Nubians of the present darker type and negroes or semi-negroes."[37] Of course, this is nonsense since Africans have always come in many complexions. Furthermore, these so-called *negroes or semi-negroes* appear in no concrete manner anywhere in Africa.

In another passage in a similar vein MacMichael says "I am strongly inclined to think that the Nobatae (Nubians) were once lords of the Bayuda and the country south of it and that their negro ancestors may have previously ousted the Libyan races therefrom, or, more probably, become fused with them in race."[38]

This is not enough. MacMichael is afraid that the Africans who ruled Egypt were "of the same stock as these negro ancestors" of the Nubians. Perhaps the most creative use of obfuscation occurs in the following passage:

"One may say then that when the Muhammadan Arabs invaded Lower Nubia in the seventh century A.D. they found there a race radically compounded of predynastic Egyptian and cognate Hamitic elements blended with dynastic Egyptian and Libyan stocks and deeply and repeatedly modified by forty centuries of dilution with Negro blood."[39]

Four thousands years of "dilution with Negro blood" means that whomever the people were they possessed the characteristics of the so-called Negroes. If any "blood" was diluted it was the "blood" of the original Africans on the land. All other people were invaders. Furthermore, when the Arabs arrived in Kemet, not Nubia, in the 7th century AD they found Africans.

Even the early Basil Davidson could not avoid the use of the "negro" illusion. There was no other racial denotation it seems for him at the time. Thus he writes "These people, these 'negroes' (for neat racial pigeonholes have little application here), undoubtedly multiplied in the years after about 5000 B.C."[40] Fortunately, Davidson lived long enough to correct most of his early references to "negroes" for the African people in all of their varieties may be referred to by their ethnic or linguistic names, i.e., Yoruba, Buganda, Sao, Igbo, Wolof, Fula, Balondo, Akan, Ewe, Mande, and Bamenda, rather than by imposed designations such as Hamitic, Negro, and Bantu. These Eurocentric determinations alienate and distort the historical achievements of the African people. Numerous other Western writers have fallen into the same intellectual cesspool.

Albert Churchward essentially led freemasonry into a disconnection between African history and civilization. Although he did not go as far as his brother, James Churchward, in finding the earliest civilizations in the mythical Mu, he laid out a situation where the "negro" theory and other false ideas such as the "Masaba negro" and "Nilotic negro," became constructions of reality that made it impossible to consider Africa as the absolute origin of human civilization. He could argue for it being "the first in evolution but never becoming the first."[41] These concepts have no real basis in science. Africans of a particular geo-cultural region can be spoken of but not in terms of Eurocentric illusions. Unfortunately, although the English poet Gerald Massey influenced Churchward he was still fundamentally a racist who believed that the evolution of the human race ended in a convergence with European man. Thus, this escape from the reality of Africa's contribution to human civilization, as *homo sapiens*, not as "pre-totemic" humanity is a false corridor to nowhere. More than three-fourth of *homo sapiens'* life was spent on the continent of Africa and there are people who have never left the continent, thereby spending the entirety of their existence as *homo sapiens* in Africa.

Khaldunic Ethnocentrism in History

Viewed from the vast field of history Churchward can be seen as a part of a larger stream of historians, beginning with Khaldun, who misunderstood and misrepresented Africa and Africans. In *The MuQaddimah: An Introduction to History,* Ibn Khaldun wrote that Sudanese "are in general characterized by levity, excitability, and great emotionalism. They are found eager to dance whenever they hear a melody."[42] Furthermore, the Egyptians are said to be like the Sudanese, Zanj, and Abyssinians for they "are dominated by joyfulness, levity and disregard for the future." Khaldun spends considerable time citing stereotypes about the Abyssinians, Zanj, and Sudanese only to report that all the stereotypes he had heard remain "inconclusive and unproven."[43] Yet in his own Arab sense of dominance Khaldun felt the urge to restate the unproven reports.

Khaldun's history does not consider the presence of African civilization in Egypt (Kemet) at all. He begins his analysis with the Greeks thus laying a foundation for Western historians to ignore the Kemetic foundation of Greek civilization. We are, therefore, left with Khaldun's incomplete and imprecise history as a basis for much racist propaganda. In addition, Khaldun's ideas on historiography underscore the significance of writing an episodic history that sets the stage for the dichotomy between prehistory and history. More contemporary scholars have seen Africa in a different light both in terms of the richness of its archaeological record and the abundance of its narrative histories.

HISTORY/PREHISTORY

It is pointless to utilize the Khaldunian notion of history and prehistory where history only begins with writing because there is a sense that prehistory contains nothing of significance to human civilization. Too much of Western history is essentially the history of the written record. We know, of course, that the African record in what is called prehistory is extensive and fruitful for an understanding of contemporary societies. In Africa there is un-limited evidence of early human development. There is also the fact that methodological and disciplinary questions raised by ar-chaeologists might be answered by the African record. In newer works, scholars are beginning to appreciate the antiquity of the African record.

The archaeologists and pre-historians of other regions have much to learn from the African record, not only from its unparal-leled evidence for the earliest periods of human development, but also methodologically. Because most of Africa has undergone en-vironmental change on a scale that is relatively minor when com-pared with the glaciated regions of Eurasia and North America, abundant data are fairly easily available to aid the interpretation of prehistoric subsistence practices. Africa also provides excellent opportunities for contrasting the testimony of archaeology with that of linguistic and oral historical studies, and for interpreting the meaning of rock art in the light of the belief systems of re-cent peoples.

I mean the definitions of history and prehistory cannot turn on the pejorative attribution to societies rich in other than writ-ten evidences. Much data exist in Africa from oral narratives to cemeteries to fabric designs to festivals and so forth to assist in organizing a cohesive record of human civilization. Indeed, Phil-lipson says prehistory may not even be appropriate a concept for Africa.[44] The period of time before written history is conventionally known as prehistory. The term is not entirely appropriate for Africa, for a number of reasons. First, there were long periods, especially in the northern part of the continent, about which written records, although available, are not generally informative on many aspects of contemporary life. There are also numerous instances where the only available written records were produced by outsiders and frequently given an incomplete account of matters that the writers did not properly understand. These are situations that confront pre-historians in many parts of the world, but they give rise to particular problems in some parts of Africa because of the generally shallow time-depth of indigenous literacy.

A different approach is required to those aspects of African culture that, to a very large extent, take the place of written literature in other regions. These include the developed oral traditions that, in many societies, preserve the accumulated wisdom of the people, including details of past history. Again, language itself plays a large part in determining a people's or an individual's sense of identity. Where written examples of ancient languages do not exist, much can be learned through the study of present-day linguistic forms and distributions concerning the nature and interactions of past populations. Beyond this, however, is a more pointed conceptual problem. The criterion of written transmission of knowledge as history is problematic because,

> "The acceptance of the criterion obliges historians, perplexed by "preliterate" societies, to exclude a large number of non-Western

cultures from history. The conceptual cleavage, pre-history-history, leads Western historians to assert the ahistoricity of these cultures in the contemporary epoch!"[45]

Preiswerk and Perrot recognize that history as taught in the West is essentially the history of the West with appendices to other peoples. They have, therefore, proposed a distinction between *History* and *history*.

"We believe that History means the classic narratives, particularly in textbooks, which come out strongly on the side of the West, and omit nearly everything that might enhance other cultures. In short, History is ethnocentric. We spell the word with a capital "H" in order to indicate that it is still predominant. It is this representation of the past, at least according to the analysis we made of the texts, which is taught to one generation after another in Western countries. It is History that appears to be perfectly integrated with the underlying ideologies of industrial society. In this respect it performs a legitimizing function both of perpetuating this society and justifying the type of relations established with other societies."[46]

Yet Africa remains central to any discussion of human society and the methodologists seeking to establish an entry into any field of human development in an historical manner must consult the African evidence. That evidence may be found in many places. Principally, however, it is the oral record that is most important in order to explore African traditions. The function of the oral historical tradition in African societies tend to be to support the state, to give official explanations of events, and to preserve the accepted versions of the group's history. In addition to the oral traditions which contain official records of various societies, the fossilized evidence of these societies has really only begun to be explored. Areas of central Africa, Zaire, Uganda, Malawi, and Angola remain to be fully studied in connection with human society. Recent research has established beyond a doubt that 7 million years ago the first so-called hominids appeared in Chad in Central Africa. Virtually all the important fossils that illustrate early origin of hominids come from Eastern or Southern Africa. *Australopithecus robustus* and *Sahelanthropus tchadensis* are regional African hominids because the first is found in South Africa and the latter in East Africa.

Discussions of hominids and oral traditions are not unrelated and do not occur in a vacuum. I am insisting on a perspective that allows us to create new ways of seeing data. One can best do that by boldly adapting an Afrocentric openness to a method grounded in seeking location. Disparate pieces of information are only seen as such when we are unable to see the disciplinary idea in the method of analysis. The questions posed by the prehistory/history debate are reoriented and located properly when we look through disciplinary eyes. This is why Afrocentrists have insisted that Africology is a discipline where one has to demonstrate a determination to pursue a particular protocol and methodology with the intention of discovering new ways of examining phenomena. By demonstrating knowledge of the methodology and a steady sense of determination the writer can lay down the principles upon which he or she can be judged by analysts and critics. How do you become a model of the discipline if you do not show that you can render the method in an exemplary fashion? Everyone can see that here is little difference between reading and writing at the level of conceptualization because the Afrocentrists who writes is the same person who reads and assesses if the writing of another is methodologically sound. In a word, my writing in this text is a demonstration of my attachment to a method.

If I had claimed that my method was interdisciplinary then I would assert a topic, not a method, and in making such an assertion I would be holding to themes and topics and subjects. For example, African American Studies is topical; it is not disciplinary; the same can be said for Africana Studies or Black Studies or Women's Studies, they are grounded in an interest in the topic, not in the approach. This is what distinguishes Africology. It is a commitment to a method. I believe that it is true as others have said that axiology rather than method links texts in interdisciplinary study, not method. The Temple School of African American Studies out of which emerged the discipline of Africology did not emphasize interest, topic, or theme, but rather how one chose to examine the particular topic and theme. Our texts are linked by the same discipline as expressed in method, procedures, and language choices.

CHAPTER FOUR

Asserting A New Cultural Situation

LANGUAGE AS A BASIS

There are at least 2,000 separate and distinct languages in Africa, making it the most linguistically complex continent. Yet no more than forty African languages have more than one million speakers, only fifteen languages have more than 20 million speakers. Therefore, on a continent where the majority of people speak at least two languages and some even as many as six, the development of new trade and commerce languages has created various pidgins, Krio, maShona, Igbo, Yoruba, Mande, Pidgin English, chiLuba, in addition to the widely accepted *lingua francas* such as Swahili, Lingala, Fanagolo, and Sango. The colonial languages of Arabic, English, French, Italian, and Portuguese are also widely used by the elites in government and civil service.

The first attempts by Europeans to classify African languages were based on their structural myths about Africa. Consequently, they gave names to a basic classificatory scheme that emerged from their frame of reference with Europe at the top of a hierarchy where Africans were at the bottom. Such irrational ideology unfortunately governed their classifications.

Sigismund Koelle collected word lists for 150 West African languages in 1854 from his base in Freetown, Sierra Leone, and derived eleven language groups. About forty languages were beyond his ability to classify. He could not place them in his scheme at all. Only a couple of groups exceeded fifteen languages. Nevertheless, Koelle is generally credited with laying the basis for Western linguists to see the large Mande speaking population as a language family covering areas in Mali, Guinea, Senegal, Sierra Leone, and Liberia.

Wilhelm Bleek, in 1862, tried to demonstrate the unity of the "the people" in most languages. As Bleek was doing with "Bantu" so the French linguist, Ernest Renan, was trying to do in East Africa. Renan coined the terms "Hamitic" and "Cushitic" to refer to Ancient Egyptian, Amharic, Galla, Somali, Beja, and Berber to suggest that these languages related to Ham or one of his descendants. Following the Bible he postulated that the Semitic languages and people were the biblical descendants of Shem, the Caucasians came from Japhet, and therefore the Africans were from Ham. This nonscientific thinking is at the base of much of the racism and irrationality of the current era.

Already this account was ethnocentric and chauvinist in its application of a particular cultural classification to African languages based on a sacred book not generally accepted in any African tradition or in African cultures. Moreover, these classifications were to cause constant arguments between Eurocentric linguists as they attempted to further establish a uniquely "negro" language of Africa. What they were finding was connection between African languages and whereas Koelle had come up with eleven groupings, some linguists were seeing a smaller number of groups. Another problem was that the French linguists and the German linguists, using their own languages, did not often agree on what to call the various classification groupings. Among European languages the terms for black, for example, vary. For instance, the French, for example, can use "noir," "negro," "l'Africain," or "negre" to refer to a black person, depending on shade of meaning. German does not possess the same flexibility, though both languages have created colorful pejoratives about African people. Black people, of course, in those countries have often responded in kind as a matter of retaliation, creating words to refer to racists.

COMMON CLASSIFICATIONS

The two earliest Europeans to attempt overall classification of African languages were Friedrich Mueller in 1876-88 and Karl Richard Lepsius in 1880. They laid much of the basis for the racist thinking which predominated language classifications for nearly one hundred years after them. Mueller, an Austrian linguist, created a peculiar classification of the world's languages based on a correlation of hair type with languages! In Africa, Mueller's division was as follows:

Tufted-Haired People Languages
Bushman-Hottentot -New Guineans

Fleece-Haired People Languages
Negro-Bantu

Wavy-Haired People Languages
Hamitic

Semitic

Nuba-Fulah

Such a classificatory scheme for languages would certainly not stand in the face of science for long and yet it was not without its competition as other Europeans sought to suggest their schemes. Most of these ideas were based on mystical racial ideology that consumed much of German and indeed European sciences for decades. Those Germans who took the word "Aryan" and sought their own origin in some distant galaxy called Aldebaran were nothing more than clever manipulators of words. In fact, the real Aryans were probably Persians, that is, Iranians.

Another European to try to make human distinctions was Lepsius who proposed an African language classification scheme involving three major divisions based on what he saw as a commonly held European scheme:

Semitic Languages

> Arabic, Hebrew

Hamitic Languages

> Hausa, Berber, (Fulani, Masai, Bari)

Negro Languages

> Bantu

> Mixed Negro

The preceding classification scheme exists with the inclusion of Carl Meinhof's supposed correctives to Lepsius' barebones scheme. For example, Meinhof added Fulani, Masai, and Bari to Lepsius' Hamitic group. Dietrich Westermann, on the other hand, proposed an alternative that consisted of these groups: (1) Bantu, (2) Hamitic, and (3) Sudanic. Westermann wanted to call all non-Bantu and non-Hamitic languages Sudanic. He linked the Khoisan to Sudanic and the Semitic to Hamitic.

Maurice DelaFosse and Lilias Homburger restricted Hamitic to Ancient Egypt, the Berber languages, and the Ethiopian languages. They created a class of languages they called Negro-African or Sudano-Guinean. It has also been suggested that Arabic is not indigenous to Africa and although it is very common in North Africa it cannot be considered an African origin language.

The most widely accepted classification of African languages has been the one proposed by Joseph Greenberg. He consolidated all of the hundreds of languages of Africa into four classes: (1) Niger-Kordofanian, (2) Nilo-Saharan, (3) Khoisan, and (4) Afro-Asiatic. Although Greenberg's classification has been debated by European scholars such as Istvan Fodor and Malcolm Guthrie on the issue of genetic relationship of languages, it is the critique of Cheikh Anta Diop, Mubabinge Bilolo, Maulana Karenga, and Theophile Obenga that raises the more profound questions. While Fodor and Guthrie suggest that genetic relationship of languages can only be discovered in regular phonological correspondences among them and Greenberg's supporters argue that similarities in sound and meaning in numerous instances of body parts, grammatical elements, natural phenomena and lower numbers cannot be ignored, Obenga and especially Diop contend that Greenberg does not go far enough. They suggest the unity of African languages, the genetic relationship of all African languages based on the Pharaonic languages. This is an approach supported by philosopher and linguist Mubabinge Bilolo and the Afrocentrist and linguist Ama Mazama. And so we have the basis of the first Afrocentric approach to language classification in Africa.

THE CULTURAL QUESTION AND THE PROBLEM OF CRITIQUE

There is a solid intellectual tradition of value issues being placed in the context of culture. Within the Western social sciences, anthropology, communication, sociology, and psychology, a growing corpus on culture has produced more than one hundred definitions of culture.

The Afrocentric scholar Maulana Karenga has argued for two types of culture based on the philosophy of Kawaida: *popular* culture and *national* culture. He distinguishes between these types of culture in this manner:

Kawaida maintains that it is the fact that African Americans have a *popular culture* rather than a *national culture* that stands at the heart of the cultural crisis they suffer. The problem of popular culture begins to become clear by its very definition. Popular culture, Kawaida posits, is the unconscious, fluid reaction to everyday life and environment. In other words, it is social thought and practice defined and limited by its unconsciousness, fluidity and reactiveness. By contrast, *"national culture is the self-conscious, collective thought and practice thru which a people creates itself, celebrates itself and introduces itself to history and humanity."*[1]

Karenga's idea is useful and heuristic in regards to culture and his work leads directly to the possibility of raising epistemological questions of the idea of culture as *philosophical* culture, *social* culture and *material* culture. I take philosophical culture to include the presuppositions, proverbs, myths epics and propositions that form an ideological position. Social culture relates to the political and behavioral aspects of a human group. Material culture refers to the objects, concrete, iconic, symbolic, and conceptual that constitute the visible, physical or cognitive aspects of the group. A human group or society serves as the base of cultural creation but as Preiswerk and Perrot say:

> Culture is not to be confused with society, the human group from which it emanates, and which it characterizes. Whereas society is linked to a certain area, except for collective migration, culture can "travel," can be exported. Cultural encounters are a permanent phenomenon in history, be it through war or conquest, or by means of peaceful communication. Whoever leaves his "cultural area" (missionary, explorer, businessman, teacher) can take on the role of an agent, modifying the encountered culture as well as his own, once reintegrated.[2]

The existence of culture goes along with the existence of society. We are all a part of some culture and cannot during our lifetime divest ourselves of culture. However, we possess various "cultural" identities, some more than other because of the complexity of their historical situation. One may be at the same time, a Yoruba, Nigerian, West African, and African. Charshee McIntyre has raised some interesting cultural questions about African Americans who are products of mixed gene pools, particularly African/ European and African/Native American mixtures. She has extended her discussion to South Africans called "Cape Coloreds." One must be careful not to confuse the transmission of culture with the biological transmission of genes. Yet, it is clear that cultural factors influence racial affiliation in the case of persons of mixed biological origins. If an African of mixed gene pool origin adopts European speech, dress, and terms of protocol he or she will be considered European or more European than African. On the other hand, the choice of an African language, African dress styles, and customs will cause the person to be considered African. Patricia Reid Merritt has written on culture, art and Afrocentricity and sees the importance of culture as a corrective for young people who often fail to exhibit discipline and purpose in early life. Her work has been to demonstrate the powerful legacy of African dance in the construction of identity.[3]

Race does not determine culture but because of the "proximity factor" it figures in the formation of certain cultural attributes much like age, another biological factor, conditions certain cultural behaviors. Race functions as a sort of subset of culture in some regard. As a scientific term, however, it lacks validity except in the sense of gene pools.

The real issue is whether or not Afrocentrists will run after European critics or establish their own critical instruments. The debate in the literary criticism arena has implications for those of us in other fields to the degree that the lack of clarity among our critics means that we will continue to be judged and evaluated by the theories and methods which emerge out of a white bourgeois racial supremacist universalist ideology contrary to either our culture or condition. No matter how you do it, you cannot justify a position that says Derrida, Foucault, Althusser, Lacan, and Baudrillard are somehow in harmony with the "freedom cries" of the millions of Africans in South Africa. We run smack up against a wall when we believe that there is something in these deconstructionists and post-structuralists that is similar to the revolutionary spirit of Africans fighting against racist hierarchy and oppression; the two situations have nothing in common.

The so-called decentered operations of reason are based on Eurocentric cultural assumptions. Two elements of those assumptions are (1) valorization of Europe at all times and (2) hostility to others. Indeed, Preiswerk and Perrot see the search for decentration as elusive because of valorization of Europe based on Eurocentric notions or reason and science.

> When Westerners studying a different culture believe they are rooted in reason and science, it does not necessarily follow that they achieve *decentration*. An epistemological position that limits itself to urging the adherence of the researchers to a code of scientific behavior and to a comparison of the results with those obtained by other researchers is, in our opinion, insufficient. In the intercultural context, particular care must be taken not only to eliminate distortions stemming from the researcher taken as an individual subject, but equally to measure the impact of the social origin of the researcher's knowledge. When four researchers confirm the results obtained by a fifth, this agreement does not necessarily mean *decentration*, when the five belong to the same culture.[4]

Preiswerk and Perrot are correct because they see that the primary result of the "code of scientific behavior" is to insure similarity of results among researchers of the same culture. It is the choreography, not the number of dancers in the piece that determines the results. But clearly reason and science are not the monopoly of Europeans. My intention in criticizing this view is to redirect attention to the transformation of the ideology of science rather than to undermine it.

The Afrocentric critique demonstrates that Eurocentric research advances in three directions: (1) the conferring of negative or positive qualities on others and the manner in which others are evaluated by criteria and measures promoted by one's own in-group; (2) the interpretation of one's own position as reasonable; and (3) the denigration of the other's position by refusing to recognize its existence.

Preiswerk and Perrot call the first mechanism projection and suggest that it is of major importance in the imposition of Western particularism as universal.

> ... there is projection, upon cultures other than Western, of a system of values common to the whole of the Western world. Thus, for example, in their relations with African, Asian and Indian American cultures, Westerners, whether representative of a free market economy or of a planned economy, act on the basis of fairly similar conceptions of time, work, productivity, the importance of material goods, relations with nature, family structure, the role of the young and the old in society, and the relative importance of cities and countryside.[5]

It is this problem that constitutes the need for transforming Western education particularly when it concerns other people. Projection conceals diversity and imposes an epistemological perspective contrary to the unique attributes of other people. There is also rationalization. This occurs in the literature when the European writer assumes that his or her position is the only reasonable one. Such a position fractures communication and imposes a particularism as universal. Denigration represents symbolic and consequently intellectual refusal to recognize the other. In such a methodological world the other remains invisible, not important, concealed, and irrelevant.

The scholar must be keen to these stratagems. When they appear we know that a Eurocentric perspective is likely. Mere presence of these stratagems does not indicate Eurocentrism however. The use of these stratagems is often the result of a Eurocentric outlook that obscures the diverse visions of the world. A self-relevant research project must not utilize clearly ethnocentric and male perspectives as if they constitute the total human reality.

A research project involves the researcher as the principal source gatherer. A decisive impact on the direction of the research project is always provided by the orientation of the researcher whose ambition and status are intimately connected to any project. The sum total of a researcher's intellectual projects represents in some ways an autobiography of the researcher. For example,

A political scientist who decides on a field study outside his own

culture or nation can be motivated by one or another of the following considerations: desire to prove the universality of his theory (or
on the contrary, to prove the authenticity of political cultures), to
follow a fashion, to adapt himself to changes in the foreign policy
of his country, to conform to the rules of the foundation which
supplies his research funds, to take advantage of his contacts in the
political circles of certain countries, to consolidate his position at
his university through international activities, to apply his linguistic skills or those of his collaborators, to avoid countries particularly grim from the point of view of living conditions and climate.

What the Afrocentric scholar seeks to avoid is "field projection,"
that is, the belief that one's traditional discipline contains all of the
tools necessary for the analysis of phenomena. If a scholar assumes
this type of burden he or she falls headlong into the intellectual
chasm Afrocentrism critiques in Eurocentrism; the only difference
being that instead of an ethnic group being projected as all encompassing, all-knowing, universal it is a particular field of study that
is so projected. The Afrocentrist trained as a psychologist must see
the relevance of historical methods in some areas as the historian
must see the relevance of artistic and political analysis in others.

THE PROBLEM OF PROBLEMS

One of the interesting aspects of the Eurocentric research paradigm even when participated in by African or Asian scholars is the
concept of problems, as in people who are "problems." Thus, one

finds references to "The Indian Problem," "The Black Problem," "The Mexican Problem," or "The Chinese Problem." Configuring the political, economic, and cultural situation like this, one does not see the overpowering reality that all "problems" have more than one participant. In other words, if there is a problem there is a "White-Indian Problem" or "a White problem with Indians" or "a Black problem for Whites or White problem for Blacks." But to study "problems" this way suggests a reorientation of research so that we raise questions of dependence, domestically and internationally. If we do this we introduce another level of inquiry that reaches the core of the Eurocentric concern with place and status. That is why, of the Eurocentrists, only the Marxists have raised such questions of domination and class. They have not raised it in reference to European culture itself and consequently remain safely behind the facade of the universality of their cultural position. One of the greatest disappointments with the Marxists is that they cannot step beyond Europe as universal symbol for standards for analysis. But to be sure they have seen the impact of hegemony and hierarchy in ways that allowed them to bequeath to the postmodernists and postcolonialists some of the same inclinations; however, it is to the Marxists that we must attribute most of these critical insights despite the fact that they are dancing on the same broken planks of Eurocentric hegemony.

In recent years the work of other European Eurocentrists have leaned toward Afrocentric scholarship, sort of winking at George

Sefa Dei, Ana Monteiro Ferreira, Ama Mazama, and Yoshitaka Miike, in passing. For example, it is clear that Boaventura de Sousa Santos has benefitted from the work of the Afrocentrists, much like it was clear that Martin Bernal had learned from the Afrocentrists, but it is also clear that Sousa Santos falls into the Eurocentric trap of assuming some superior claims for Europe. The inability to divest himself of privilege sits at the door to his complicated presentation of his view of globalization and world sociology. At the University of Coimbra, the most prestigious university in Portugal, Sousa Santos has created an aura of mysticism around his conclusions that the South, that is, the Intellectual South, must be considered in any discourse on knowledge. Yet his problem is that he has not revealed what he knows about African culture, history, or social institutions. For Sousa Santos the South remains only India and South America. If Africa is mentioned, it is only to ornament, not to convince or to describe in any deep structural sense. One should not deride the attempt of Sousa Santos to seize the European conversation but he won the Advanced Grant of the European Research Council (ERC) in 2011 with the express purpose of creating a project *ALICE: Leading Europe to a New Way of Sharing the World Experiences* to reframe the discussion about globalization. Despite his impressive credential of having worked with CIDOC, Ivan Illich's institute in Cuernavaca, during the time of my visit there in the 1970s, although I do not remember him, his work appears to be an iteration of the hegemonic European word to maintain control of global discourse. Thus, it is not so much Europe alongside others as it is a temporary tactic to allow the South to express itself before Europe reassumes its position of dominance. I think that reading Sousa Santos' *Epistemologies of the South* one can see that his emphasis is different from mine in *Facing South to Africa*. My essay is toward Africa specifically for the reason that other writers often leave out any discussion of the voice of Africa. Sousa Santos promises hope but does not deliver the fundamental need to uproot racist culture in the West and throw out the social sciences that have not brought us any closer to world peace or communal harmony. We ask, "Can't we do better?"

Most of our problems are solved through the use of functional concepts. They assist us in organizing, selecting, classifying, and defining objects. The Afrocentric scholar examines reality by structuring it on the basis of philosophical and functional concepts. As we interact with facts concepts emerge, not in a miraculous manner, but out of the interaction between the scholar and knowledge. Preiswerk and Perrot speak of mono-cultural, inter-cultural, and cosmo-cultural concepts referring to those which serve one culture, several cultures, and all cultures, respectively.

What we discover is that an African concept is often different from the European or Asian concept even though the same term may be used. Take the example of the term "son." In Africa if you ask a man with a young boy alongside him, "Is that your son?" He may answer, "Yes, this is my son." But when you ask him, "Is that the son from your wife's womb?" He may answer, "No." To which you may say, "Then that is not your real son." Of course, the man would contest your statement by saying that "He is not from my wife but he is truly my son." Obviously, if the man is Asante, Ga, Yoruba, or Igbo, he has a different concept than a Westerner. Clearly the categories do not coincide. For the European there is a fundamental difference between an adopted son and a "real" son. For the African, a member of the family automatically succeeds the deceased father and becomes the "real" father, in no way conceptualized separately from the "physical" father. There are neither adopted sons nor orphans. Furthermore, those known in the West as nephews can also be sons. As we know one can give numerous examples of the fallacy of transferring concepts from one culture to another without accounting for difference. Preiswerk and Perrot say,

> In Western societies, orphans are children who have lost a father, a mother, or both parents. An anthropologist seeking to determine the number of "orphans" in an African society will doubtless come across individuals whose situations correspond to this state of affairs. And yet, the society under study does not necessarily know the term orphan, for according to African tradition the juridical status as well as the psychological condition of an "orphan" do not correspond to those of Europe. There is therefore no reason to distinguish an "orphan" from other children, or to create orphanages.[6]

When an American or European says that Africans have no concept of time actually they mean that the people have no concept of time in the European sense of lineal, chronological time. It is incorrect to say that Africans have no concept of time; the concept of time is well developed among Africans. If they did not have a concept of time, then planting, harvesting, and festivals would be erratic and without organization in African society, and we know this is not true. Since African societies are highly structured in terms of regularized rites, festivals, and agricultural behaviors, time is an important concept to Africans and the calendar is an African invention that dates back to its Nile Valley origins on the continent. Climatic and ecological determinants assist in the assignation of days, weeks, and months to various activities but in no case is the concept of time ignored.

Nonwhite and non-European are concepts that distort the reality of Africans. Europeans often define others by the absence of a phenomenon specific to their culture. This is a self-centered topology where, for example, an economist may speak of market societies and societies without markets or societies with writing and societies without language. This topology describes what a society is not rather than what it is. Thus, "nonwhites" becomes a term without meaning when applied to Africans or Asians. We do not say robins and thrashers are "non-sparrows."

Use of nonwhite or non-European places the European in a position by which others are measured as being either-or. But knowledge of the African is limited because we do not have specific reference: he is, in effect, non-something which makes him, definitionally, nothing. Almost no European writer would be so callous as to say that Europeans are non-Africans.

All knowledge is a continuation, acted upon by numerous scholars in the quest for some portion of truth. Although we might assume that there are many versions of an event, in reality they are extenuations and attenuations of the same knowledge. No knowledge remains the same and as soon as it is written or spoken it becomes the foundation for future knowledge. One only has to look at the vicissitudes of history to see how ideas have gone through transition depending upon the era and the scholar. When nationalism is important the historians emphasize patriotism; the Marxists highlight class distinctions; and moralists see corruption

> ...experts amuse themselves in measuring "psychological modern-
> ization" among Africans by using the following criteria: modern
> conception of time, placing the accent on the future; a positive
> attitude toward government activities; a sense of optimism and
> control over one's destiny; patriotism; belief in determinism and
> scientific knowledge; a trusting conception of people; a positive
> attitude toward the leaders of the country, and de-emphasis of
> traditional beliefs.

Again the aim is to force Western criteria on African societies. Furthermore, the assumption that these criteria are not possible or probable in Africa means that the researchers have projected an image of African that often does not have basis in fact. It is much like the illusion of the "negro" discussed elsewhere in this book.

Moreover, the idea of modernization is self-topological anyway, suggesting that Africans should become like Westerners. Conceivably Europeans might have something to learn about modernization from Africans!

Sciencing

In the United States, for example, a number of communicationists have worked on the discourse style of African Americans in an effort to reveal the fundamental African orientation of that style. What they have shown both lexically and syntactically has been the African base of much of our language. Notions of word play, signifying, the dozens, riddles, proverbs, and *sciencing* are related to the search for harmony—the flight towards cosmic union often referred to as mysticism. *Sciencing* is particularly interesting because of its generative power.

Sciencing is the interpretation of a word by using its contemporary constituents as clues to its political and cultural meaning. According to the scholar Maulana Karenga, *sciencing* grew out of the rhetorical motif of the Moorish Science Temple, an urban-based nationalist religion with origins in 1914. As a popular analytical instrument among religious and cultural orators, *sciencing* has a strong tradition in political rhetoric. The African American speaker who uses *sciencing* is on familiar ground and can find sympathetic audiences who have grown up in the African American church which is actually the incubator of many of the rhetorical flourishes one finds in the American society.

Some Sciencing Terms

history	his-story
negro	knee-grow
solar	soul-ra
justice	just-us
community	come unity
imagination	image of a nation
America	A mir-a-cle
Africa	Af-ra-ka
disco	disk company
chemistry	khem is thee
Israel	Ra is God
Research	search again
Obama	O bomb mo

In *sciencing* each of these terms become useful to the person making an analysis of the political condition of African Americans. Africology cannot escape a concern with *sciencing* as a functional aspect of discourse because it is out of the elementary uses of *sciencing* that the communication is able to achieve a greater degree of knowledge. I recall the first time I heard a discourse on Columbus "discovering" America. It was a lecture given on the corner in Harlem when I was a young adventurer in the 1960s. The speaker, whom I never knew, explained that instead of revealing anything about the Native Americans, Columbus "covered" their history and what we needed to do was to "uncover" this "covering" called "discovery." Quite frankly, the logic of the street-talker was not Aristotelian but it was real, fleshy, truth to us. The evidence that "sciencing" may have had an impact on the discussion in the public on this subject is clear to many African Americans. The argument is more sophisticated now but no more correct. Let us review the situation.

Numerous Western textbooks are filled with the idea of geographical discovery of African or Asian or American lands. One can find instances where a writer says Mungo Park "discovered" the Niger River or Columbus "discovered" America. In both of these cases two points are significant. The first is that ethnocentrism is clearly present when the writer assumes that a European "discovered" a place where other people already lived. This ethnocentrism leads to the next point that is an emphasis on the lack of historicity of the indigenous people. Selection of facts becomes a series of judgments claiming to be facts but in reality are accepted opinions. Indeed, epistemologically, what has been presented as an "objective" fact reveals itself as a value judgment, which implies the intrinsic superiority of one mode over others. It is not a question here of knowing whether there is real superiority or not, but to be aware of the valorization inherent in the choice of facts and concepts. The "discovery" phenomenon is widely employed in reference to Europeans in Africa. The names read like the who's who of the *National Geographic*: Livingston, Speke, Park, Moffat, Stanley, etc.

In reality, the first discoverers and explorers were the people of the East African valleys that discovered mountains, new valleys, rivers, and ways to traverse them as they left their original home. They discovered fauna and flora from place to place and discovered what was edible and what was poisonous. They discovered fresh water lakes and saltwater fish. They observed and recorded first the movements of the universe. Primary discovery, if anything, has to do with the first humans viewing geographical phenomena and passing this information on to others. Thus the first African to see the mountains of the moon, for example, passed that knowledge on to others making it possible for them to record in their minds the location and character of the phenomena. Therefore, the scholar must be careful in writing about discovery since so much history is laced with hostility toward Africa. The early European Egyptologists, writing principally in the nineteenth century, Europe's arrogant age of exuberance, were particularly hostile toward Africa. Discovery, even in a sense of civilization, was said to have come from some supposed relationship of Egypt to the Indo-European civilization. Of course, this has been proved grossly inaccurate. But the move to subvert Africa's place has been consistent and antagonistic. Even if we use "discovery" in the sense that it is used when people say "Columbus discovered America" we are employing a positively Eurocentric imposition. It is not even certain that Columbus was the first European to arrive in the Americas. We now know that Africans reached the Americas more than one hundred and fifty years before Columbus. Ivan van Sertima's *They Came Before Columbus* and Michael Bradley's

The Black Discovery of America show that Africans arrived in the Americas long before Columbus. In the end, our own "sciencing" leads us to the discovery of knowledge. Carter G. Woodson and Asa Hilliard have provided the Afrocentric paradigm with critical interpretations of what Western education does to African people. Carter G. Woodson provides us with a general discussion of the entire educational enterprise. He is particularly keen in his analysis of what the received educational model teach African American students in colleges run by African Americans. Those colleges, like their white counterparts, are responsible for the miseducation of African students because they valorize European knowledge but attempt to devalue African knowledge.

According to Woodson, the teachers of the students were at fault because:

> "These "educated" people, however, decry any such thing as race consciousness; and in some respects they are right. They do not like to hear such expressions as "Negro literature," "Negro poetry," "African art," or "thinking black"; and, roughly speaking, we must concede that such things do not exist. These things did not figure in the courses that they pursued in school, and why should they? Aren't we all Americans? Then, whatever is American is as much the heritage of the Negro as of any other group in this country."[7]

He contended that the "seat of the trouble" is in attitudes:

> The "educated Negroes" have the attitude of contempt toward their own people because in their own as well as in their mixed schools Negroes are taught to admire the whites. The chief difficulty with the education of the Negro is that it has been largely

imitation resulting in the enslavement of his mind. Somebody outside of the race has desired to try out on Negroes some experiment that interested him and his coworkers; and Negroes, being objects of charity, have received them cordially and have done what they required. In fact, the keynote in the education of the Negro has been to do what he is told to do. Any Negro who has learned to do this is well prepared to function in the American social order as others would have him.[8]

What he knew was that the education of African was nothing more than a device, an instrument of control from without. The promoters of such education could stand back and laugh at our gullibility in supporting the cause of the oppressors. Blacks are boxed in an educational framework that creates exiles of rebels and persistent resisters. Woodson feared that the real difficulty in educating black people stemmed from the passing on of white biases to blacks. Taught from books of the same bias, trained by Caucasians of the same prejudices or by "Negroes" of enslaved minds, one generation after another serves no purpose but to imitate whites. In other words, a black teacher instructing black children is in many respects nothing more than a Eurocentric white teacher thus engaged; in each case the program is about the same.

Asa Hilliard's advances in Afrocentric interpretation are made in the identification of strategies for miseducation. Where Woodson gives us a philosophical perspective, Hilliard demonstrated how the educational systems of the West conspired to keep African people ignorant of themselves. Here are some strategies that Europeans have often used to distort African realities.

Temporal Tampering:

This means presenting European facts as if they preceded their African antecedents, when in fact they did not, for example, Hippocrates before Imhotep, the Parthenon before Ipet Isut.

Isolated Text:

Choosing to focus on isolated European incidents as history while ignoring African history, e.g., Livingstone and Stanley in Africa.

Creating Illusions:

Claiming the existence for something that does not exist, e.g., *Negro, tribes, Sub-Sahara Africa.*

Name-Calling:

Identifying Africans who defended their lands as "warlike" or calling Khoi-San people "Bushmen" or "Hottentots."

Asa Hilliard's original developments in this area have taken on new vigor by the Temple Afrocentric School. A generation of scholars has followed Hilliard's guidelines and activities in their own pedagogical and methodological work. Younger scholars such as Michael Tillotson, Reiland Rabaka, Serie McDougal, Christel Temple, and Ibram Rogers Kendi, among others are writing their way into the history of Africological scholarship from a centered perspective. They are just the vanguard in a movement of Afrocentric scholarship that continues to advance the field of Africology. A fully equipped field of African Studies driven by a strong disciplinary Africology will lead the renaissance in African cognitive behavior. This must be intention of all African social scientists such as Ndiaye, Muhwati, Gwekyewere, Sesanti, Moyo, Diagne, Gumede, Babutunde, and all those who have declared to me their commitment to a new African vision.

RALPH ELLISON AND THE VISION OF INVISIBILITY

Ralph Ellison, perhaps more than anyone, took the miseducation of Africans as the basis for a profound novel. Prior to 1960 Ellison was the most famous black writer in the United States. He had succeeded in overcoming the shadows of Richard Wright, Paul Laurence Dunbar, and Langston Hughes, and was massively worshipped by the white reading public. He remained little read by the black community and soon the people turned to James Baldwin and then to Toni Morrison. But it is worthwhile to look at the role of Ellison. What Ellison did with the idea of a people brainwashed by the entire society, even African American institutions, was to show how we had become victims of the society and ourselves. *The Invisible Man* was published in 1952 and won a National Book Award.[9] It was the literary equivalent of Harriet Beecher Stowe's *Uncle Tom's Cabin* in that it served to focus attention on the African presence in America. The novel focuses on an idealistic Southern black man who recognizes the limitations of the social, economic and political he was expected to play, but only after his directness and assertion had destroyed his college career and ultimately jeopardized his life. In New York, where he moved when his Southern experience proved futile he discovered his invisibility, that is, discovered that to whites he is invisible. Even the communists, despite their rhetoric, view him as a token. The situation is pointless—he decides to live underground in a Harlem cellar. Briefly, the *Invisible Man* is the narrator of the novel but several other characters figure in Ellison's array of witnesses. The *Grandfather* never appears in the novel but he has left the invisible man with a deathbed riddle that becomes a driving force in the work—a motif of the necessary. Ellison's book brought attention to many issues in the black community. The narrator says he is an "invisible man." This is so not because he is physically invisible but rather that people do not see him. He lives underground and burns 1369 light bulbs while listening to Louis Armstrong's "What Did I Do to Be So Black and Blue." Living underground the narrator tries to write his life's story. As a gifted speaker he is invited to give a talk to a group of white men. They give him a scholarship to a black college but demand that he participates in a battle royal with other young black boys as a form of entertaining the whites. They are blindfolded and put in a boxing ring. Soon the white men have them scramble on the floor looking for fake gold coins. The idea is to humiliate young black men. When he gets to college he is asked to give a white trustee, Mr. Norton, a tour of the campus. Norton tells the narrator about his daughter. He then listens to the story of Jim Trueblood, a poor black man, who had impregnated his own daughter. Norton was so overcome by this story that he needed a drink and when they got to the bar, the Golden Day saloon and brothel, a fight broke out among black veterans. Norton appeared to be unconscious and finally a black veteran tried to help him but actually condemns Norton and the narrator for their lack of sensitivity to race.

Reverend Homer A. Barbee, a blind preacher, gave a talk at the college praising the school's founder. The school's president, Dr. Bledsoe, criticized the narrator for not showing the white trustee the better parts of the black community. He then expels the narrator and gives him recommendations for jobs in New York. The founder of the college resembles Booker T. Washington. He knows how to play on the minds of the Southern whites—their guilt and pride. Dr. Bledsoe is the president of the college and he believes that a black person can only succeed by being a hypocritical liar. If the white man asks how are things? You tell him, "fine," even if you are dying. If the white man says, "you seem happy," you say, "I am" even though you are crying.

Soon the narrator lands in New York only to discover that the recommendation letters said that the narrator was unreliable. He finally gets a job at a paint company whose slogan is "Optic White." The narrator serves as an assistant to Lucius Brockway, the black man who creates the white paint, but Brockway is suspicious of the narrators and thinks that he is joining a union. The two black men fight, and with no one watching the paint-making machine it explodes and the narrator is knocked out. He recovers in the hospital where the white doctors conduct electric shock therapy experiments on him. When he leaves the hospital and regains his memory someone suggested that he stays with Mary, a woman who teaches him about his history and culture. He gains consciousness of his condition living at Mary's house. Brother Jack listens to a speech that he gave and then offered him a job in the Brotherhood. This job helped him to repay Mary for her hospitality. He meets youth leader Tod Clifton and Ras the Exhorter who reject the interracial Brotherhood and believes that blacks should fight their own battles. The narrator makes dynamic speeches and becomes a prominent figure in the Brotherhood. Brother Wrestrum accuses the narrator of trying to use the Brotherhood to advance his own selfish ends. While a committee of the Brotherhood investigates the charges, the organization moves the narrator to another post, as an advocate of women's rights. After giving a speech one evening, he is seduced by one of the white women. The Brotherhood encounters lots of disintegration and is rife with suspicion The narrator finds eventually tracks down Clifton and finds him selling dancing "Sambo" dolls. Clifton does not have a permit to sell on the street. White policemen question him, hassle him, and attempt to arrest him and after a short scuffle they shoot him dead. The narrator sees the whole thing with his own eyes. He holds a funeral for Clifton and gives a eulogy in which he portrays Clifton as a hero. The Brotherhood is angry with him for holding the funeral. Ras sends Brotherhood people to beat up the narrator. However, the narrator becomes involved in the riot going on and then sets a fire to a tenement building. As he is running from the scene he sees Ras who is dressed as an African king. He asks other people to lynch the narrator who escapes and encounters two police who believe that he has loot in his briefcase taken from the riot. He falls down a manhole and has lived underground since. The end is the beginning of the story and he is ready to emerge and take his responsibility to the community. Hambro, a white supporter, is the advocate and philosopher of the integrated Brotherhood. Tod Clifton is a popular leader of the brotherhood and friend to the invisible man. Ras, is a militant and separatist, who resents blacks who associate with whites. Rinehart is a Harlem character whom the reader never meets. He floats in the narrative as a presence never seen. With this host of characters Ellison weaves a mighty novel, an epic of its time. His artistic consciousness is at the peak of his time, his poetic language is forceful and his ability to provide cohesion brilliantly displayed. I think the time focus here is the tragedy of an individual, however sensitive, to lose out against the demonic forces of a warped society. Ellison highlights the individual against the collectivity—he thrusts the individual plight of the invisible man out front as an element of modernity. In this sense this is a modern novel, written with the sensibilities of a thoroughly modern man: I mean Ellison's symbols are those of the "modern" writer. But one cannot read this work without some reference to Trayvon Martin and Michael Brown and scores of other African American young men who have found themselves victims of police violence. It is easy to ask if the crime of Mumia Abu Jamal and Assata Shakur was really their survival after altercations with police. Had they been killed then the narrative would have been one of invisibility of a different sort. However the real point has to be that the modernity of Ellison does not betray his attempt at telling the truth as he saw it.

My own critique of Ellison is grounded in Afrocentric philosophy. Essentially I contend that the African American writer ought to be centered in his or her culture. To do otherwise is to become marginal, peripheral. This is true, or should be true, for all writers since the American culture is not a completed project and we all have our historical legacies. The reason for this has to do with the overwhelming power of Ellison's symbolic prose. He draws on Sophocles, Homer, Dostoevsky, Freud, Jung, Burke, Eliot, Joyce, and Malraux for the texture on his novel. He combines these images with symbols from Richard Wright, the blues and spirituals, our epic story, and personal experiences. Like jazz riffs, some of these symbols and allusions trail off in a disappearing act—you see them and then you don't; Ellison is in the symbolist tradition of

Melville and Hawthorne and perhaps the more vernacular tradition of Hemingway and Twain.

This is a problem for me, not so much for Ellison, and certainly not for the novel that is, as we have come to accept over the years, a remarkable literary feat. I find the *Invisible Man,* in some senses, a truly African American book, a *tour de force* of the multi-faceted, many-sided, and polyrhythmic nuances of the African way with all of its percussion, syncopation, and energy. I like what Ellison does in this novel with that approach but I don't believe he had the faintest idea that he was using an African form. The only way I can know this is because of the subsequent impressions he has given—the idea that he is simply a writer, that he owes no allegiance to Richard Wright, who truly understood his roots and the use of African and African American

On another point, Ellison is brilliant. He shows that the anchor the invisible man has is his own folk tradition; perhaps a tradition that Ellison might want to question. One should not try to get away from the magical quality of the folk tradition; this tradition inspires the novel and gives it rich texture with themes, images, myths, and symbolisms. The invisible man finds his enlightenment, his truth, as he finds his blackness. His movement up is when he plunges into a dark manhole. The rhyme from the folklore "If you are white, you're alright; if you are brown, stick around; if you are black, get back," appears throughout the novel.

In the end, however, this is not a novel written for black people—it uses the vital images and creative allusions of African people in the U.S. to tell a poignant story to white people. I do not mean that we do not accept its brilliance but it is a distorted, twisted, marginal reality—in the final analysis, though gifted with a style and flair, and capable of mastering the novel as form—Ellison is not writing this novel to me however much he uses my African American materials. His aim is to write to a white audience, to show them this invisibility of the African, and if possible to create thought, guilt, understanding, and liberation for the white man.

But the African is invisible because of the hostility toward Africa and Africans. The African disappeared in America, except in the constant Pan African circles of black activists and intellectuals. Ellison speaks about an invisibility caused by the attack on Africa and he does not know it—there is a manner of seeing in this novel that loses sight of the real audience for a writer, his own literary community. But for the African American writer it is confusing because he or she often feels compelled to write to the "white" audience. A white writer that can simply write from a cultural view that is simply considered natural experiences no such constraints. Were Ellison to have written to a black audience because he knows that this would be his primary reading public he would have quite different experiences.

The invisible man tells his story with a combination of style, irony, and wit. There is also absurdity as he views his trials as adventure. To compensate for his propriety he strings his underground hole with 1369 light bulbs, gets five phonographs to hear the blues properly, and listens to Louis Armstrong's plaintive "what did I do to be so black and blue." In the end he discovers he is who he is—but that brings to mind the question asked by the African philosopher Frantz Fanon in talking to African people, "Who are we?" Fanon saw a profound identity crisis confronting the African as a result of five hundred years of European domination—the wonderful aspect of this novel is that Ellison tries to establish **in** the mind of his reader the territory that belongs to the African. He chooses the battle royal, the dozens, chitterlings, pig ears, mustard greens, the subway, spirituals, folklores, and blues— above all else this is a blues poem, an expression of a condition, a will to escape, even if that means making yourself invisible by living underground.

By the 1960s and early 1970s the African wanted visibility— assertiveness was the order of the day—Ellison had inadvertently contributed to the possibility of understanding the anger of the black masses. Black power and black is beautiful became common phrases and bonding terms. If black was now beautiful, then the color ought to be worn so others could see it.

Visibility was a rejection of invisibility, a rejection of the back-of-the-bus, a refusal to go along and a return to our historical and ethical center. Indeed, we captured the moral ground, the high ground. Our escape into the subterranean environment of America had denied what we had. So no question could be decided without reference to our struggle. The assault on the American conscience has always been an ethical assault. How can you accumulate trillions of dollars of wealth on the basis of free and extracted labor of Africans working from "can't see in the morning to can't see at night" and not have any semblance of decency around any number of social or academic or economic situations? One hundred million Africans were uprooted in the European slave trade and exported to the Americas. Twenty five million died in ships, in dungeons, or by committing suicide—there never has been a national cleansing of this vast example of international criminal activity—it is this situation that sits at the back of Ellison's novel.

The African American came to school with an unusual heritage—having come a great distance in such short time against incredible odds. Remember the slave had no rights, no right to hire self out, to marry, to make contracts, to plan her or his own time and could be punished at will. To make me go away—me as the symbol of the culpability of those who looked for the apotheosis of whiteness in a white supremacist world—I was to disappear—the African had to become invisible—he couldn't be seen—all public places either denied our existence or said we didn't matter, the literature omitted Africans as the idea was to forget. In the process, we have also forgotten but in our forgetfulness we have lost the meaning of our present situation. Our invisibility must never again be assured. For the sake of this nation, the African presence and the meaning of it with all of its nuances must be seen as a peculiarly American response to the European slave trade. The writers who speak in the tradition of Ellison assure the impossibility of our invisibility in culture, art, the sciences, cuisine, history, literature and music.

Ellison recognized our flight toward cosmic union as a sort of mysticism, not magic which is entirely different, but mysticism, mediated by myth, narrative myth, working itself out in our collective lives as part of a larger context. The human nature, our nature, must be in harmony with the environment in order to be at peace. Unlike magic which seeks to control nature and the environment demonstrating an avidity for power and mastery, mysticism unites us with the invisible through the visible as we become in an Ellisonian sense whole again.

TUNING TO THE COSMOS

The ancient Egyptians held that humans reflected the deities and that the best moral position was to be in tune with the cosmos as governed by the deities. Although the classical priests recognize certain unique capabilities of humans they saw humans as part of the same cosmos as animals. A special relationship existed between humans and other animals under the power of the deities. In fact, humans are expected to be in harmony with the forces of the universe. Thus evil and good are not oppositional in human nature but appositional, a reflection of the internal harmony of the universe itself. The ancients were students of nature. And as students of nature they analyzed the conditions of men and women from observable facts.

Therefore, the modern debate as to whether humans are essentially good or evil did not occupy the minds of the classical priests. They were sure that humans possessed both good and evil. If one assumed that humans were essentially good and tried to attribute evils in history to social causes he would be begging the question because humans are truly at the root of most evil tendencies in history. If one assures that man is essentially evil he is questioning in a way that show he is not "essentially" evil because he would not be able to reach such a conclusion if he were. Actually, the quality of the being that judges self in such a remarkably direct way is without question one of uniqueness in character.

I shall not go further with the discussion of the classical African views except to point out that anthropocentric attitudes were more extensive among the ancient intellectuals than they are today when we know that neither our planet, sun, nor galaxy is central to the cosmic immensity of the universe.

THE QUESTION OF MARXISM

Classical attitudes are discovered in the myths and sayings of African people to the extent that the interconnectedness of humans to ecology, environment, community, and universe reflects the worldview of Africa. Afrocentricity contends that human problems become problems when humans no longer appreciate the connectedness to nature. One can follow the path of these problems in Marxist formulations as well as any other. Afrocentric critiques are possible in every sphere and of every ideology.

Marx's revolution in economic thought occurred largely because he re-conceptualized the social relations that made possible commodity production in bourgeois capitalist societies. He rejected the idea, advanced by some economists, that crises of economic systems were the results of formal possibilities. Rather he contended that the crises of the economy in capitalist societies were manifestations of all of the contradictions of such societies; in fact, the crises would recur because they were systemic. What is introduced in social relations, therefore, is a markedly materialist project.

In short, the recurrence of the overproduction of capital led to the overproduction of commodities that meant that they could not be sold and therefore produced an economic crisis. This presented a new mode of social relations in the European world. Prior to the capitalist "evolution" crises were produced because of natural constraints such as floods, famine, plagues or war that caused use-value underproduction. The capitalist mode, on the contrary, overproduced exchange-values. In the first situation, that is, in the pre-capitalist mode people produced what they used, underproduction of what was necessary for use, whether due to plague or war, meant an economic crisis. In the capitalist system the idea is to produce for exchange-value usually money, and when there is overproduction the system experiences a crisis.

Marx argues that under capitalist economics the material production process is inhibited or constrained from producing use-values because of the pressure to produce exchange-values. What is clear is that in addition to constraints on material production such as nature, labor productivity, and resource scarcity, the capitalist emphasis on production for creation of more exchange-values inevitably leads to a crisis.

The social relations are constrained because material productions of society are separated from the laborer who generates production. In effect, material production becomes value production and this transformation throws the capitalist and laborer into opposition, conflict, because of their relative positions in the production process. What Marx suggests is that a correlation exists between the contradictions inherent in the production imperatives of exchange-value seeking and relations of production as defined by the work of the laborer. Thus, a class division exists between the capitalist and the laborer.

Material production is inseparable from exchange, distribution, and consumption. Marx did not analyze production independent of social relations and institutional parameters in which exchange and distribution occur. Therefore, the material production and social relations must be seen in their totality.

In the end what Marx does is to reintroduce a unity into eco-

nomic theory as it relates to Europe by showing a historico-genet-
ic relationship of the basic forms that make capitalist production
possible. He restores the relationship between the laborer and
material production in an explication of capitalist production as a
whole and engages in a discussion of the forms of value, commodity, and money. Two points must be made at this juncture.

My critique is not based on a fundamental rejection of Marx's
analysis of capitalism but rather on the inability of Marx to see the
interrelationship of culture and economics. Although social relations are central to Marx, by social relations he means essentially
economic relations, not cultural relations. To be sure, in one sense
all cultural activities are social relations but in an Afrocentric use
of the term "culture" I mean the generative expression a people's
myths, motifs, and celebration of their history. Economic relations become the results of cultural relations, the most elementary of human expressions, e.g., religion. Afrocentricity totalizes
cultural, economic, and social organization, demonstrating the
essential character of human society from the centrality of Africa
and the primacy of the classical civilizations.

The second point is based on the Marxist's hierarchy of social
and economic organization: communist, socialist, capitalist, mer-
cantilist, feudal, and communal. What this Darwinist concept of
evolution does is to reserve for the "highest" forms of economic
and social organization the white European nations, whether East
or West. All of the African systems would be, almost by defini-

tion, on the "lowest" step of the hierarchy. This is unacceptable as a way of looking at the world.

Much of Marx's own thinking was based on Hegel and Feuerbach. He particularly used Hegel's philosophical premises but extended his intellectual reach beyond philosophy to include history and economics. In fact, MacIntyre says that while Marx was conscious of the need for a new departure in philosophy he kept returning to Hegel, even despite his differences with Hegel on such issues as the origin of the state and of society and the rationality of the state as expressed in constitutional monarchy. Both Marx and Hegel, however, find their sources in the European examples, which is correct and essential, for European writers.

It is the extension of Hegel's Prussian examples to other parts of the world and Marx's European examples that must be carefully scrutinized. While Prussian despotism is akin to Ugandan despotism or South African despotism, they do have different cultural characters. This much I am sure even the most Eurocentric writers would admit. The one fact exemplified in all of Marx's analysis is that human beings are not resigned to their fate; situations can be changed. In his case, where the exploitation of labor by capital had warped social relations it had to be the workers. In our case, where a distorted Eurocentrism, with its religious transmutations in apartheid and white supremacy, projects a false view of human history and culture, it must be challenged by a progressive, disciplined Africology.

The need for this severe critique of the Marxist hierarchical categorization of society and societies lies in the European concept of the ascendancy of Europe. Marx obviously was no less a victim of his environment on the conceptual issue. Hegel, of course, was a racist. Marx's own intellectual growth began when he wrote his doctoral thesis on Epicurus' transformation of Democritus' atomic theory as a part of what happened to Greek philosophy after Aristotle. Marx saw that Greek philosophy turned from speculative to practical, from metaphysics to ethics and, of course, his own problem was to turn Hegel's speculative ideal philosophy into concrete practice. I am not troubled by Marx's analysis of capitalist theory. He finds a problem and seeks a solution. The troubling aspect of most Eurocentric research, however, Marx included, is that it fails to consider the origins, the bases of knowledge. There is no indication that Marx ever considered the fact that Greek philosophy is derivative in many respects from Kemetic philosophy in Africa. A closed European intellectual practice has permitted the European to avoid coming to terms with African civilizations that pre-date Greek and Roman civilizations by thousands of years. This is seen in Marx as well.

There is also the continuing cultural question with which Marx finds difficulty. Our answer, both to the cultural and economic questions, draws intrinsic value from an Afrocentric analysis of the cultural and economic questions facing Africans. Therefore, while Marxism's answer to the cultural question may be nonex-

istent, Africological studies demonstrate rather straightforwardly
that an Afrocentric response to this issue is based on the *categoral*
paradigm, loss of terms, a fundamental metaphor for both economic and social explanations of the African position vis-à-vis
the Western world. European slave traders moved Africans off
of physical terms; missionaries and settlers moved Africans off of
religious terms; and capitalists moved Africans off of economic
terms. This metaphorical conception of the human, African, reality is clearly at the heart of any reclamation process. To reclaim
a centered place in economic, social, or political contexts, the
African must first find centering in a cultural and psychological
sense. To be moved off of one's terms is to be a victim of aggression, whether physical or mental. The conscious behavior of the
African must be one of seeking to return from the margins and to
regain terms.

In many respects only Sartre was bold enough to refuse to
identify Marxism with the writings of the post-Marxists or with
Communism in the old Soviet Union. The so-called "black super-
Marxists" made no such distinction since a respectable part of
their philosophy has always been tied to a rejection of capitalism
rather than an acceptance of the freedom. The existential freedom
that exists within each of us to define ourselves, to construct ourselves, and to resolve our problems does not compromise us. This
reality exists because we are presently engaged in its fulfillment.

Among the African American socialists John Henrik Clarke

stands out as the one proponent of freedom who exercised a judgment or made a decision to see culture as the most relevant aspect of a generative approach to socialism, to freedom with all of its explosive significance. Clarke's early role as an associate editor of *Freedomways* solidified his socialist credentials while creating an enormous amount of speculation about his intellectual commitment to Marx. As the dean of African nationalist historians, John Henrik Clarke, was celebrated by an entire generation of younger scholars such as Walter Rodney, Leonard Jeffries, Ronald Walters, Marimba Ani, James Turner, and Charshee McIntyre. The commitment of these authors tended to be to the idea of Africa-centeredness rather than to any dogmatic Marxism. Indeed, the Guyanese intellectual and activist, Walter Rodney best typifies this pragmatic socialism in the service of Africa. Others who respected Clarke and socialism such as Cornel West and Manning Marable attempted to humanize the sharper edges of a Eurocentric ideology. However, it was the African studies of Clarke that saved him from the ignominious fate of a person divorced from his cultural center.

The shift in Walter Rodney's intellectual orientation began with a break in the strict Marxist-Leninist terminology which one sees in some of his earlier articles. One senses that this development was the result of his concern with the Diaspora question and his closeness to the methodological principles found in systematic nationalist as presented in the works of the African

Americanists, particularly Kwame Ture (Stokely Carmichael), Maulana Karenga, Malcolm X, and others. What is fascinating is that even before his teaching stint at the University of Dar es Salaam, Rodney had attained a remarkable relationship to the nationalist position, which although not purely Afrocentric was within striking distance of the concept. In other words, Rodney had already absorbed quite a lot of the systematic nationalist position. In "Grounding With My Brothers," a speech he gave on many occasions in the United States and the Caribbean, Rodney maintained a strong nationalist orientation. He was able, perhaps more than any of his contemporary African-Caribbean scholar writers, to link his intellectual objectives with the work and aspirations of Africans in the United States and on the continent of Africa. Indeed, *How Europe Underdeveloped Africa* was a socialist analysis with definite systematic nationalist sentiments. But even so, Rodney did not make the leap to an Afrocentric position. He provided a solid analytical basis for uncovering how Europe had disrupted the continent beginning with the slave trade and continuing through colonialism. For Rodney's fundamental insistence on the Marxist position excluded from the beginning his acceptance of a truly Afrocentric analysis which would have gone further than Marx to demonstrate that the African nations had essentially been moved off of their own economic centers, interests, and were serving the interests of the European *metropoles*. This is not to say that Rodney would have denied the legitimacy of the

Afrocentric analysis; it is simply that he injected the class analysis in such a way that European methods prevented him from making the further leap to the centrality of Africa in interpreting African phenomena. Thus, Rodney leaves relatively untouched the issue of the mental incarceration of African people.

Yet we see in Rodney's speeches and pamphlets a growing concern for systematic nationalist and Pan-African issues. It is unlikely that a scholar as consistent and persistent as Rodney in his main political and epistemological concerns could have shifted to a more systematic nationalist position in this way had there not already been present in his intellectual position certain assumptions and predispositions favorable towards the methodological opening afforded by systematic nationalism.

Like Rodney, Frantz Fanon was interested in the critique of subjugation and dehumanization.[10] He spoke for Algeria and Martinique, Africa and the Caribbean, about the fear, inferiority complexes, servility, and despair of those who have been oppressed. The inexorable reasonableness of his stance and eloquence of his passion placed the dialectic of racism and counter-racism on an irreversible course of conflict. His analysis of the African's response to racist oppression became a major work about colonial neurosis. While Rodney had come to his systematic analysis from the Caribbean and Britain, Fanon came to his position from the Caribbean and France. Both were victims of racism and psychological violence.

Frantz Fanon was on the path to an Afrocentric view of history. Although he understood and grasped Marx and Lenin, he was not a Marxist in any common sense. He did not subscribe to the theory that the working class of Africa was revolutionary. Nor did he believe that the European working class would support Africa. In fact, he even regarded the Western proletariat as unsympathetic to the colonized people of Africa. In taking this position, Fanon articulated the Afrocentric view of Marxism: the impossibility of Marxists to incorporate into their thinking the dimension of white racism. Proletariats of the West enjoyed the benefits, even held their places, at the expense of the colonized workers of Africa and Asia.

Fanon grew up in the Martinique of Aimé Césaire. Since Martinique was a department of France he volunteered for the French army and served in Europe. Between the years 1945 and 1950 he studied medicine at Lyons and edited for the Black Student Caucus a paper he called the *Tom Tom*. In 1951 Fanon completed his dissertation in medicine and wrote the powerful *Black Skins, White Masks,* which sought to look at the psychological ravages that affected colonized Africans. Fanon's fortune as a result of his analysis was his appointment as the head of psychiatry at BlicaJoinville Hospital in Algeria about the time the Algerian Revolution began. Because he was convinced of the rightness of the Algerian struggle he found himself increasingly in conflict with the French authorities. He assisted the rebels for two years and finally had to resign his post at the hospital. Fanon could not find peace on the sideline of history and so after the First Congress of Black Writers and Artists in Paris in 1956 he decided that he would take up an editorial post on the FLN newspaper *El Moudjahid* in Tunis. This led him to further involvement with African Liberation ideology of which he was to become a principal theorist. Although he begins *Black Skin, White Masks* saying "I am talking of millions of men who have been skillfully injected with fear, inferiority, complexes, trepidation, servility, despair, abasement" by the time of his death at 36 he was speaking *for* millions of Africans—in the Caribbean, in the Americas, and on the continent. We had all become his audience and those of us who were students in the Sixties saw him, even in his death, as the prophet of the age.

David Caute placed Fanon's political resistance in the intellectual tradition of a charismatic prophet when he wrote "Karl Marx was 'created' by capitalism; Garibaldi by Sicilian poverty; Lenin by the Russian aristocracy; Gandhi by British imperialism; Fanon was created by the white man." This is not correct. Fanon was created by *les Damnes de la Terre*, or *The Wretched of the Earth* who were victims of white oppression. To say as Caute says that he was 'created' by the white man does not say enough. Indeed, the revolutionary impulse in Fanon was directly related to increased knowledge of the conditions of his people. He became a restless revolutionary activist whose militancy had led him to participate in the Algerian Revolution but had reached its full power in his political writings.

Unfortunately, Caute is too busy trying to place Fanon in the Western Marxist tradition to see the essential African response to oppression that he makes. While at thirty-six he had not fully developed an Afrocentric ideology, he was most surely on his way. Caute's misunderstanding of Fanon leads him to the conclusion that Fanon would not have understood Malcolm X or Marcus Garvey. Indeed, everything in Fanon suggests the opposite. Since Fanon's ideological developments were inspired by Césaire, a vigorous anti-racist, his path was the same as the anti-racists in the United States.

I visited Martinique in December 2013 and talked to the ordinary people of the land to understand their relationship to Césaire and Fanon. What I discovered was ambivalence; I was much more capable as an outsider of appreciating the impact of these two giant thinkers than those who knew their warts up close. However, like other Eurocentric writers, Caute seeks to claim even the contributions of the most significant political philosopher of the 1960s by saying that all Fanon did was in terms of the European revolutionary tradition. Of course, Caute assumes that there is neither another tradition nor another revolutionary people. Both assumptions are wrong.

There is in Fanon a major step toward the Afrocentric methodology. His work bears an essentialist, abstract character that seeks to strip bare the rhetorical nature of white propaganda. In this sense, Fanon's style is much like the essay style of James Baldwin who was a better essayist than novelist. Fanon speaks without ambiguity about "the black," "the white," "bourgeoisie," "colonized," and "peasants."

The Afrocentric method confronts the Eurocentric viewpoint on moral grounds and demonstrates its vacuity in race relations, the primary field of interaction with others. For whites integration means that the African must become like the whites. Whites also believe that they must accept Africans in order for integration to work. Any Afrocentric analysis must dispense with this position because it is theoretically and intellectually vapid. There is, as James Baldwin noted in *The Fire Next Time,* impertinence on the part of whites to assume that they must *accept* Africans. The thought has never occurred to them that the African may not have agreed to accept them.

Fanon found in his assault on colonialism a method for liberating the self. As a political activist Fanon was keenly aware of the individual consciousness was intricately linked to collective consciousness. His training in psychology and psychiatry had prepared him for a psychoanalytic analysis of the African's situation. To understand this situation with all its nuances and complexities it was necessary to study the neurotic structures of individuals.

Fanon did not see the African's quest for psychological and political liberation in following the European. In his view the white man had become the principal producer of destruction. "When I search for Man in the technique and the style of Europe I see only a succession of negations of man, and an avalanche of murders?" It is as the Afrocentrists claim a Europe dripping in the red blood of insistent racism flowing from the wounds of the masses of African and Asian people.

Therefore, the Fanonian method of revolution against white colonization is both a rejection of Europe and an act of violence against oppression. This takes a national and activist character in as much as colonization is violence itself; it must be violently rejected. He sees violence as a form of positive, humanistic self-assertion against oppression. It is the self-asserting itself as human against an inhumane system. Thus, the lack of will to assert against such a system is tantamount to accepting one's status as victim.

The success of the violent confrontation with colonialism rested on three factors according to Fanon: (1) The will of the colonized people to liberate themselves, (2) the fact that colonies were markets for the oppressor nations and protracted war disputed markets, and (3) the fact that the colonial powers feared the communists would infiltrate the national resistance. He believed that under such conditions the use of violence would succeed. Indeed Jean-Paul Sartre had written in the preface to *The Wretched of the Earth*, "The native cures himself of colonial neurosis by thrusting out the settler through force of arms. When his rage boils over, he rediscovers his lost innocence and he comes to know himself in that he creates himself ... to shoot down a European is to kill two birds with one stone, to destroy the oppressor and the man he oppresses at the same time."

Jean-Paul Sartre captures Fanon's essential point in the drive for liberation. In Fanon, method is the internal, centralizing force of the oppressed reaching toward freedom. He writes, "at the level of individuals, violence is a cleansing force. It frees the native from his inferiority complex and from his despair and inaction." Since the process of colonization radically changes the colonized, violence is to be expected, in fact, it is necessary for psychological liberation for the colonized to resist oppression with equal violence. For Fanon, Gandhi's methods were inauthentic forms of decolonization; nonviolence never permitted the oppressed to "win" freedom, and "struggle" itself must never be confused with violence for the nonviolent practitioner. Yet everything the oppressed is fighting against is violent.

Revolutions are short-term affairs. Human emotions last a long time. Violence that results in the killing of human beings is problematic as a liberating ideology apart from the moment of the action. Killing the barbaric racist haunts the liberator; but in the end he sees no other way out of his situation. Indeed those who participate in the liberating violence are few in numbers compared with the beneficiaries. How do we go about liberating *their* minds? This is the dilemma of African governments that have seized power politically but have not gained control over the cultural or educational lives of their people. This is different from taking over control of institutions. Unquestionably schools and broadcasting stations can be controlled and governed but what is taught and what is broadcast is as important, perhaps more so than merely governing.

The prosecution of a revolution never touches every individual in a society. And violence is a solitary experience even in collective action. This is not to say that Fanon is totally incorrect in his assessment of the psychological impact of violence on the oppressed. We cannot assume the same situation for those people who are not oppressed. Furthermore, random, non-directed, anarchic individual acts of violence would not be considered either therapeutic or valid in Fanonian terms. My only point is that it does not always happen that the African cures him or herself of psychological dependence on Europe by thrusting out the settler. Sometimes the settler's culture lives deeply within his soul.

Fanon's ideas were grounded in the resistance tradition of African intellectuals. As a socialist, he was, like Malcolm X, an enemy of white racism, capitalist exploitation, and psychological oppression. Fanon found that revolution demanded a critique of domination much like Malcolm would later discover in his analysis of African experience in America. Although Fanon never succeeded, as Malcolm was to succeed in identifying the underlying force of exploitation and oppression as white racism, he was clearly writing *in* the tradition established by Martin Delany, Marcus Garvey and Du Bois.

PSYCHOLOGICAL QUESTIONS

Frantz Fanon could identify psychoanalytical interpretations as the basis for understanding the complex situations affecting the victims of racism. How did the African interpret in her skin the economic and social inferiority thrust upon her? Fanon maintained a critical posture toward Freud, arguing that "the neurotic structure of an individual is simply the elaboration, the formation, the eruption within the ego, of conflictual clusters arising in part out of the environment and in part out of the purely personal way in which the individual reacts to these influences." In this passage, Fanon demonstrates an appreciation for the Freudian attitude toward the anomalies accompanying those who have been victimized but he finds difficulty in reconciling various psychological traditions with his attempt to synthesize economic and psychological determination. Although both Freud and Jung have some influence on his work, particularly in terms of theories of sublimation, childhood sexuality, and the collective unconscious, he is not a child of their psychology but rather an Afrocentric precursor.

Like Fanon, we recognize the importance of both Sigmund Freud and Carl Jung who are among the most significant contributors to the European language of social sciences. Terms such as repression, *id, ego, Oedipus complex, occultism, extrasensory, alchemy, reaction formation, collective unconscious, rationalization, libido, persona, anima, animus*, and *supereg*o have become intertwined with the everyday Western way of thinking.

Sigmund Freud was to psychology what Albert Einstein was to physics. He altered the terms of Western psychological discussion and presented a new vocabulary. Freudian psychology clearly delineated a conception of the person not usually found in African thought. His view of human nature was pessimistic. His idea of the human race was not exceedingly optimistic due to the enormity of social ills that beset the world. Being born into an irrational world Freud believed that humans could only pass on their irrationality. This irrationality, according to Freud, was based in the nature of human personality. The basic systems of the personality are the *id*, the *ego*, and the *superego*. According to Freud these systems should be in harmony if a person is healthy but because they are often at odds the person must work to adjust them. If they cannot be adjusted the person becomes angry with himself and the world. According to Freud the id provides fulfillment of the pleasure principle. This principle assists the person in eliminating tension or maintaining tension at a constant level. The ego is governed by the reality principle that, according to Freud, meant the postponement of the discharge of energy until the actual object that will satisfy the need has been discovered or created. The ego has to be able to tolerate tension until it can be appropriately discharged. The superego is the judicial branch of the personality. The superego represents the ideal and strives for perfection, not reality nor pleasures. When a person's conscience comes into play then the superego, the moral keeper of the personality, has been activated.

The Afrocentrist finds little in Freudian views with which to be pleased, largely because Freud was uncomplicatedly interested only in the Eurocentric enterprise as universal. Furthermore, as John Henrik Clarke observed, Freud's notion of the relationship of sexual dysfunction to sanity could not be validated by the African experience. As Clarke said, "People say they have good sex lives but remain crazy and dysfunctional."[11] Perhaps Carl Jung's theories were more akin to those of the Afrocentric School because of Jung's attempt to understand the wholism of the cosmos.

Jung was Freud's premier student but broke with his mentor during the publication of his major book, *Symbols of Transformation*. Eager to pursue his own line of thought, Jung delved into the occult, astrology, and human symbols. He travelled to Africa, visiting Tunis, the Sahara, Kenya, Uganda, Sudan, and Egypt. He learned Swahili in order to perform word-associations with his African colleagues. These experiences and others in Asia and among Native Americans in New Mexico gave him a broad view of human personality not found in Freudian psychology.

What Jung wanted to know was how symbols, language, dreams, and visions, revealed the collective unconscious of the mind. He discovered that the unconscious manifested itself in the occult, dreams, symbolisms, and myths. Because he used whatever sources existed to assist in discovering truth Jung was often considered unique to other scientists. In this respect, his methods were similar to those of the Afrocentrists who insist on using oral sources, symbols, fabrics, linguistics, botany, animal husbandry, and religious icons to establish the truth about a human situation.

The human personality, according to Jung, is shaped by archetypes, the original model after which other things were patterned. He said there were many such archetypes: fire, a ring, God, birth, death, the hero, demon, earth mother, and power, to name a few. Four archetypes are of such importance that Jung devoted great attention to them: persona, anima, animus, shadow, and the self.

The persona enables one to portray a character that is not one's own. It is a mask worn publicly with the idea of presenting a good image. The anima and animus are the "inward" forces of the psyche as opposed to the "outward" force of the persona. This inward force is called the anima in males and the animus in females. The shadow contains more of man's basic animal nature than the other archetypes. Jung saw it as the most dangerous of all the archetypes because it is responsible for the best and worst in humans when dealing with those of the same sex.

The self is the organizing principle of the personality. It is like the sun in the solar systems, organizing, unfixing, and supplying the entire system. As the structuring mechanism the self unites all parts of the personality. Jung's work has implications for Afrocentric inquiry because he shows how we might utilize the traditional thought of African "psychologists" for guidelines to understanding African culture. For example, Jung is no more significant for the Afrocentric scholar than Anokye, called Okomfo Anokye, who lived in Ghana during the seventeenth century. Anokye helped to construct a set of concepts that applied to the spiritual kinship. Thus, *okra, sunsum, ntoro*, and *mogya* represent the major components of the individual. The *okra* is a person's destiny or mission; *sunsum* is character, genius, morality. *ntoro*, from one's father is personality; and *mogya* is blood that one inherits from his or her mother.

What neither Jung nor Freud nor very many white psychologists deal with is the psychopathology of white racial supremacy itself. The presence of African culture has been so firmly established in the Diaspora and on the continent, both as *continuity* and *tradition*, the need to defend Africa, if it ever existed, does not exist. On the other hand, the need to find explanations for white racial supremacy thinking remains a major task of Africologists and other scientists.

The valorization of whiteness is profoundly a five-hundred year-old Eurocentric enterprise. To engage in a discussion about white supremacy is to employ a term used by whites to legitimize white control over others or to speak about the control exercised by whites over others since the 1600s. Both are political uses of the term "white supremacy." Since white supremacy, in a biological sense does not exist, writers who use the term are using a theoretical construct based on economic, social, and political situations enforced by the military power or the threat of violence.

The term "supremacy" does not enter the literature from the African or Asian side but from whites themselves, thus even the critical European scholars were inclined to use the term when debunk-

ing it. From a strong psychological base in the minds of Europeans
of the seventeenth-nineteenth centuries the idea of European superiority was cultivated and grew into a mature notion of white
supremacy by the twentieth century. Three hundred years of steady
European domination of the world had given the Europeans a serious psychological problem. Accompanying the political and economic "successes" of colonization was the seeming capitulation of
other people's cultures to that of the European. This led Europeans
to the belief in the superiority of their culture, history, economic
systems, child-rearing practices, communal organization patterns,
art, and architecture. The political manifestation of this was the
exercise of a vision of white supremacy. Even the most "progressive" and ethical circles in the European intellectual community
insisted that Europe was or should be supreme. Drunk with the
intoxicant of racial supremacy the European ethos, as seen in the
literature and social relations, exhibited an intense racial psychosis.

Frank Tucker's important essay on *The White Conscience,* written in 1968 but little reviewed and pretty much dismissed by the
scholarly public, remains one of the few serious historical attempts
in America at the critique of the European domination of the
world for the last five hundred years. Tucker's documentary account of the history of the West shows how Europeans dehuman-
ized themselves and distorted their own values by exercising brutality against people of color. Indeed, J. J. Ingalls had said in a speech
to the United States Senate in 1890 that "The race to which we

belong is the most arrogant and rapacious, the most exclusive and indomitable in history. It is the conquering and the unconquerable race, through which alone man has taken possession of the physical and moral world. All other races have been its enemies or its victims."[12] Nearly a hundred years later the Canadian scholar Michael Bradley could write that the white race is most responsible for the pollution of the atmosphere, the great catastrophes of the earth in war, and most of human suffering caused by racial discrimination.

Even in the debate over the humanity of others, the Eurocentric view shows arrogance towards others. When Montezinos denounced the Spaniards' treatment of the Indians in 1512 he had one major convert to his position, Bartholeme de Las Casas, later the Bishop of Chiapas, who was to take up the case of the humanity of the Indians. Sepulveda and Oviedo, two theoreticians of the conquistadores, argued that the Indians did not have nationality and were by nature slaves. But the Indians neither questioned theirs nor the whites humanity. That they were different goes without saying but that hardly constituted a case for questioning humanity. In this regard the European notion of who was and was not a human was a self-serving definition. Las Casas and Alonzo de la Vera Cruz argued that the Spaniards were taking Indians' lands and reducing them to slaves. Indeed Hanke reports that Las Casas even thought the Indians could make better Christians than the Europeans. Almost all these early European race theorists took it for granted that "the original man" was white and degenerated to become Africans and Indians. Rebecca Cann's work has now shown that, if anything, the mother of those of us living today was a "black woman."

In a far-reaching laboratory experiment with mitochondrial DNA samples drawn from one hundred and forty eight individuals from around the world, Cann demonstrated that structurally all living human beings are descendants of one woman who lived in Africa about 200,000 years ago. Indeed, Cann and her colleagues substantiated the fossil work of the anthropologists such as the Leakeys and others. Africologists like Diop, Yosef ben Jochannan and Obenga had concluded the African origin of civilization through signs and symbols of primordial human beings as well as the legacies of science and philosophy found in the Nile Valley. Rebecca Cann's work gave a biological interpretation of human family-hood. In view of this work it is logical to assume that we are all African. Establishing African origins should not lead to an inevitable biological determinist line that argues nature is never modified by the environment. Apart from African origins, however, some scientists have contended that the genes are responsible for all human behavior and culture. Indeed, this line of thinking takes Darwinism to a new level.

SOCIOBIOLOGY AND CULTURE

As an extension of the biological determinist line, sociobiology declares the genes holds culture in a basket. Edward Wilson, the "father" of sociobiology, argues that every aspect of our behavior is directed by our genetic endowment. Wilson's view that natural selection, artificial selection, and sexual selection are the principal pathways to genetic endowment has influenced almost all of the sociobiologists.[13] Rosenberg's *Sociobiology and the Preemption of Social Science* raised profound questions for the study of human behavior in the traditional framework.[14]

What has become most important in the articulation of the sociobiology project is the evolutionary, and by that I mean, Darwinist construction of human emotions, ethics, impulse, problem-solving, and symbol making. Such a construction might be taken to imply that human beings are not responsible for their behavior. The sociobiologists see the problem in such a construction and posit the "hypertrophy effect" which when combined with the "multiplier effect" permits a small genetic trait to become a major social behavior. Thus, moving from genetically determined behavior to social or cultural behavior is not only possible; there are certain hypotheses that help to explain how it happens. When the genetic trait crosses the threshold it becomes social behavior. Of course, as in social science, so in sociobiology, we are discussing concepts, theoretical possibilities, analogies, and metaphors that cannot be precisely measured or explained. Whether this threshold effect exists or not is not the Afrocentric question but rather what are the implications of a theory that could lead to dominant influences artificially redesigning or engineering genes for political and social purposes? Here we must walk carefully or we will return to the past with a more sinister approach to controlling human conditions.

Other approaches to human emotions and values have been credited with providing different assessments of human achievements. In effect, the progressive Western notion of human rights with its roots in eighteenth century British and French culture dominates the discussion of political freedoms. Sociobiology aside, the idea that human society is ordered according a preset hierarchy appears to be central to the European enterprise. Thus, one sees that the human image, in all of its peculiarly Western formulation, whether as it relates to human rights or to human image, appears reflected in the shadow of social or political hierarchy.

RE-EXAMINING THE KNOWLEDGE QUESTION

Arthur Lovejoy's *Great Chain of Being* expertly totalized the Western cosmological concept of human beings![15] Plato and Aristotle are considered the originators of the Great Chain of Being concept. In *Timaeus* Plato advanced the idea of the Demiurge who is responsible for creating a world outside one's self. In the working out of this cosmological framework European writers saw themselves—that is, Europeans—as the highest link in the human chain.[16] This was neither the case with Plato nor with the nascent European culture. To the West prior to the coalescing of Europe in the minds of a few regional writers of the seventeenth century, the ascendancy of this European thought reached its climax in the lectures of Hegel whose views on Africa and human rights fell clearly within the hierarchical ideal of Europe. We are, therefore, under obligation to examine the Western idea of the human image.

Josiah A. M. Cobbah has written in "African Values and the Human Rights Debate: An African Perspective" that even the Western notion of human rights has to be questioned!" In his penetrating article, Cobbah contends that the Africans who have written on the issue tend to follow the Western paradigm. These authors are necessarily tied to the popular Western notions they have been taught by their teachers. Thus, "while the increase in the discussion of human rights in Africa is both timely and refreshing, a survey of the literature leaves one with the impression that scholars proceed on the assumption that although traditional concepts on the enhancement of African dignity are present in African culture, African societies have become modernized to a point where a discussion of these traditional concepts has become esoteric, or indeed a pretext by Africans to avoid the hard questions about human rights violations for which the Western world expects convincing answers."[17] Cobbah clearly delineates the problem in the ethical individualism of the Western world by demonstrating that it is tied to notions of benevolence, heroism, and sacrifice rather than to the natural duty not to harm one's fellow. He is explicit that "supererogatory acts" emanate from ethical individualism's idea of charity and goodwill, rather than the African communalism worldview. Thus, the human rights notion of the Western world, based on an Anglo-American construction of ethical individualism, is even different from the view held by a minority of Western scholars in the scholastic tradition. The international advancement of the Western idea in human rights has imposed a European natural rights perspective that denies the right of those in "need for sustenance and society's obligation to satisfy this right." Cobbah's attempt is to posit an Afrocentrist's view on the issue of human rights without resorting to the biological determinist position taken by many with white racial supremacist doctrines. What we see is that race is an illusive idea when it comes to the issue of human rights with its philosophical foundation firmly based in culture. In a more recent study of human rights in Africa, Clyde Ledbetter has demonstrated that there is a strong indigenous idea of the dignity of the human in Gambia but that it has been complicated by the interference of European and Arab ideas.[18] Neither the Holy Bible nor the Holy Quran was holy to traditional African societies and hence they are interventions into the cultural agency of Africa.

A Question of Racism

Several recent scholars have challenged the general methodological line on race taken by liberal and conservative writers. Elisa Larken Nascimento has demonstrated the illusive nature of the discussion on race in the literature of the Americas and Europe. Liberals in Brazil and the United States often treat racism as prejudice or some blatant expression of nastiness toward African people by ignorant white people. Of course, the issue is far more complicated than that kind of analysis. Afrocentrists see racism as a hierarchical system of privilege embedded deeply in white culture and expressed as a type of racial envy where whites seek to displace blacks in physical, mental, and emotional terms. Thus, racism remains an abnormal human system of thinking. This is why the mass leader, Elijah Muhammad, once argued that it was a natural feature of whiteness. He could not see evidence where whites consistently strove to de-racialize their thinking. In 2013 two school administrators in Pennsylvania resigned abruptly when it was discovered that the school superintendent in Coatesville, Pennsylvania, was having racist text conversations on school district supplied cellphones where they insulted blacks, Latinos, Arabs, and Jews with the most horrendous type of racist garbage one could imagine. The ensuing discussion about the incident led many to the conclusion, possibly correct, that racism was endemic to the system. However, it should be noted that these were the people who were caught because of an investigation and they had to turn over their phones to the authorities. What about those who are not caught?

Marxists treat racism as a subset of class exploitation brought about by mercantile capitalism. When you begin with the argument that class is the dominant paradigm for conflict then you immediately arrive at the conclusion that race must not matter so much in the scheme of ordinary life. The Afrocentrists know that this is false reasoning and that many people hide behind the class argument to escape the embarrassing familiarity of racism in the American society. It is easier to argue the class question and be considered on the side of progress than it is argue, as Joe Feagin has indicated, that there are white racial frames that are found deep in white America's psyche. So one may have a class problem, but it does not necessarily eliminate the abiding racism problem.

Elisa Nascimento in a study of Pan-Africanism and South America chose to examine race as a system of domination, "involving violent imposition upon conquered peoples of alien economic, political, religious, linguistic, social and cultural scientific norms and notions."[19] She makes an exceptional observation when she write that "while international monopoly capital is the operative element of world economic dominion, Eurocentrism and its attendant doctrine of white supremacy are the operative elements of world psycho-social and cultural domination." This biting indictment by one of most observant anti-racist of this era identifies the problem in the clearest light. In both instances, class and race, the African person is moved off of his or her economic and psycho-social/ cultural grounds. The imposition of monopoly capitalism and the imposition of Eurocentrism are cooperative, neither being determinative in its own right, in the negation of

Africa and African people. Therefore, we must see racism as transcending the color of skin and see it as a complex and interlocking psychosocial and economic system of domination. Thus, we have returned to the idea of the loss of terms. Africans are deprived of dignity, history, culture, and respect in such a system.

It is important that a researcher understand the complexity of the system of exploitation. Although a considerable amount of work has been done on the explication of the economic aspect of domination and increasing amounts of work are being written on the psycho-social-cultural factors, few of these works have teased out the intricate nature of racial domination. The Afrocentric scholar should be conscious of the nonracial argument in relationship to institutions. One of the more subtle forms of racism is in the use of terms like objective, neutral, color-blind, and nonracial to refer to openness of the psychosocial/cultural system. But the system is itself structured on the basis of racial stratification and regardless of how "nonracial" in approach caretakers of the system may be at the present time, the system remains an instrument of racial domination. The projection of racism by using apparently nonracial terms represents a new development in the discourse on race. Ronald Walters argues that one of the impulses of imperialism is "to create other systems in its own likeness, not only to serve its economic interests but to reflect its particular brand of political philosophy as right and virtuous by the establishment of similar institutions."[20] Walters could just as well have written of the definitional, theoretical, and methodological institutions that could be created by an invasive psychosocial/cultural hegemony. Hence, the imposing ethic establishes itself as more valuable to even a slave than his own psychological or cultural self. The absolute loss of terms at the level of one's cultural control means that culture itself seeks ways to mask its potency. The word "yes" might become "no" and "bad" might become "good." Several works have explored the Eurocentric assertion as it related to the African during the slavery era.

Progressive African American Historians Intervene

John Wesley Blassingame's *The Slave Community,* though flawed in some ways, represents one of the first historical studies to use the Eurocentric object as subject. He seeks to empower the enslaved African with a historical voice, thereby asserting the centrality of the African's experience in any discussion of European slavery. For Blassingame, a native Georgian, the life experiences of the African as revealed in narratives and autobiographies, were not just worthy of study but were essential to an understanding of the slave systems. In the Preface to his work Blassingame complains that "historians have *deliberately* (italics mine) ignored these sources." His complaint is at the heart of the problem with Eurocentric methods: they usually seek to totalize phenomena in the European experience as if it were universal. While we cannot question the centrality of the European view in matters pertaining strictly to Europe, in those matters where the European culture is involved with the culture of others we must always challenge the imposition of Europe on others. Historians, as they have come to be defined in the West, are profoundly Eurocentric in their enterprise and have been unable to consistently transcend their provincialism even while examining African realities. This is why few Afrocentric historians have appeared over the last few decades. The most that we are able to see are historians who take into consideration the intersections of gender, race and class, but they have been unable, by virtue of the discipline's Eurocentric perspective, to engage in approaches that can be called Afrocentric. I am not saying that they have to do so; however, I am questioning the imposition of Europe or the white perspective on all human facts when we know that such a limited view can never sustain a universalist approach. While Afrocentricity has never reached as Eurocentric history has reached to speak for some universal principle, it has become an important critique of Eurocentricity much like Marxism may be considered a critique of Capitalism.

Blassingame is an extremely astute observer of the historical record but often he falls victim to the Eurocentrism that affects too many of us Africans educated by whites. He writes of the Native American interaction with the Europeans like this, "Consequently, Europeans in North America either exterminated the *war-like* (italics mine) hunting tribes or worked the simple food gatherers to death." But Blassingame knows that to refer to the Native

Americans as "war-like" is incorrect and a misnomer. If any people were *war-like* it had to be the Europeans who "exterminated" or "worked the Native Americans to death."

Sterling Stuckey's *Slave Culture* and Vincent Harding's *There is a River* represent two monumental works on the nature of the African's presence in America.[21] In *Slave Culture,* Stuckey demonstrates the intrinsic value of the African's commitment to centeredness by showing that many African Americans possessed the understanding and acceptance of African culture necessary to maintain dignity and strength in the face of hardships. Harding's book, poetic and lyrical, provides a fresh narrative of the role played by the African in his and her own liberation. Taken alongside the works of Blassingame, Nathan Huggins, Darlene Hines, and Robin Kelley, the works of Stuckey and Harding constitute a historical consciousness that will ultimately lead to a new Afrocentric interpretation of African American history.

In Stuckey and Harding we see the spiritual, rhythmic, soulful method assuming the proper place in analysis. It is from these two authors that we learn about the inner workings of the African American mind in song and dance, work and play, religion and science, community and church, industry and theater. They remind us of the ancient rites, the so-called secret societies of Africa, in their efforts to uncover the causes and reasons for African American social and cultural behavior in the United States. What I mean is that they reconstitute our history, making it meaningful in innumerable ways by showing the unity of soul and method. Quite frankly, the pattern for this kind of analysis existed in the "secret societies" themselves; often the principal training schools in early classical and late classical traditional African society.

The ancient African civilizations did not separate religion and philosophy. Indeed the contributions to art, literature and the sciences are directly traceable to the religio-philosophical institutions of the Nile Valley civilizations. Expressions of this unity of religion and philosophy appeared in the construction of the temples, memorials, obelisks, causeways, and pyramids of the classical period. The finest works of architecture were based on the principles derived from ancient wisdom that dictated proportions and motifs based on the laws of harmony.

The Greeks called the classical African wisdom mysteries; the modern European writers refer to this wisdom as secret societies. Both designations are problematic. *Mysteries* is misleading as a descriptive term because the ancient wisdom was only a mystery to the uninitiated. Once a person had learned the religio-philosophical-ethical principles they were not mysteries and consequently should never have been so designated. To call this wisdom "mysteries" is to elevate the Greek conception (as outsiders) of the wisdom as a more important conception than that of the people who created it. In this regard, even the fighting hawks (a group of African American historians who rose, often from study groups, in the early 20th century to challenge white interpretations of African history) were often mistaken because they followed the Greek designation. Some of them were misdirected by Freemasonry and this aberration in their thinking frequently led to factual errors or to reliance on old European freemasons' works as authoritative documents. The proliferation of the term mysteries in reference to African knowledge might have gained impetus from this preoccupation with Freemasonry.

In Greece itself so-called mystery schools were established and some of them, like the shrine of Eleusis in Attica, contained huge spaces for audiences to see the initiates perform the rituals. The Greeks divided the wisdom into two parts: (1) *lesser mysteries* and (2) *greater mysteries*. The lesser mysteries were granted to persons of good moral character who matriculated for the training. Since the lesser mysteries were taught **in** the form of a pageant, even young children could be admitted. The greater mysteries tested the person in moral, physical, and intellectual areas. One had to be sound in body and mind and show knowledge of the acquired wisdom before one could successfully pass the test. Once a person passed the test he was a member of the order.

THE IDEA OF SECRET SOCIETIES

Secret societies is a term given by scholars to the institutions which have inherited and maintained the ancient wisdom. Observing institutions such as the '*epa,* the *gelede,* the *mbira,* the *poro,* the *nimba,* and the *abakua,* the European author used the term secret societies to identify them. But these institutions, where the arcana of the shrines, that is, the necessary knowledge for interpretation of sacred symbols and priestly writing existed, were truly societies of secrets.

An initiate learned the accumulated knowledge of the ancestors and participated in the great drama of "universal" beginning. The vows and obligations of these religio-philosophical institutions laid the foundations for establishing order, justice, peace, and ethics within the various communities. As Sterling Stuckey has shown with brilliant insight into the learning experiences of Africans in America, our knowledge, often accumulated from the ancestors who practiced many of the methods they had learned from their parents and relatives, came from participating in the great narrative dramas of resistance against oppression. And while "slave" culture was marginal in many ways to the white society, it was not marginal or peripheral in terms of the psychological and cultural caring that took place within the powerful context of Africa-centeredness. Only when scholars wake to the task of examining African lives and events from this position can we fully know what it means to regain our terms.

A slave is one who has been reduced to an artifact of an oppressor's creation and changed into something defined, fabricated, and marked by the will of another as being useful for the oppressor's purposes, thereby losing one's own material and creative terms. Only in this context can we truly understand the danger-

276 AFRICAN PYRAMIDS of KNOWLEDGE

ous implications of the loss of terms. European slavery maintained the most brutal, total, and repugnant form of human reduction transforming the "organic materiality" of Africans into what was essentially an inorganic violence.

HOW AFRICOLOGY ACHIEVES ITS END

Africology seeks to bring a new birth to the intellectual enterprise by encouraging scholarship to tear itself away from the imposition of a European domination, in fact, to place Europe in a normal context, separate from arrogance and within an arena of pluralism without hierarchy. To regain terms, Africology must remain free to challenge unquestioned assumptions about the principal issues confronting the African world. Methods must be tied to specific historical and cultural foundations, to the primacy of Kemet, and the foundations most useful are those in which the issues or subjects are centered. An Afrocentric world voice, regaining terms, will be a full, florid, whole, and productive voice, speaking the intellectual ideas of a new, generative category of human inquiry from a centered perspective. This is the only method for de-hegemonizing the Eurocentric social sciences and philosophy that have created a world of oppressors and the oppressed, winners and forced losers, and those with privilege and those without it. Asians and South Americans and Pacific Islanders and all people considered marginalize will have to have their own voices raised in order to create the chorus of human liberation.

Moreover, Africology cannot achieve its purpose as a liberating discipline unless it is founded on assumptions that dignify humans rather than negate them. This *dignification* of humans begins in a critique but it can never end in critique. Although it is true that when I have waited for a Eurocentric science that liberates humans I have been disappointed with efforts of the postcolonialists and the practitioners of *ALICE*, who are simply seeking ways to maintain hegemony, yet I should have recognized the fundamentally different approach to human knowledge in the Western project. Neither the European social sciences, namely, criminal justice, sociology, psychology, political science, anthropology and history, nor European humanities can liberate those who have been victims of cultural, political or economic domination. If anything, the oppressed are victims of the theorists who explain and interpret the condition of the masses in order to be able to more accurately "predict" their responses to an increasing array of stimuli. How can criminal justice as a discipline liberate the masses of Africans, Latinos, Native Americans and Southeast Asians, or poor whites from police brutality or the rule of a racist "injustice" apparatus? Africologists must critique but also in our research we must propose concrete actions that lead to the lessening of disharmony, oppressive situations, pain and suffering, misunderstanding, and dislocation. This means that we must create do-tanks as well as think-tanks. We must propose a new ethic along the lines articulated by Maulana Karenga, one that brings restoration and reparations, the *serudj-ta* moment, into the world. How do we recover, repair, and restore the land, the people, and the society?

ENDNOTES

PREFACE

1   Ama Mazama, *The Afrocentric Paradigm*. Trenton: African World Press, 2003.

CHAPTER ONE

1   Ama Mazama, *The Afrocentric Paradigm*. Trenton: African World Press, 2003.

2   Trent Schroyer,. *The Critique of Domination* New York: Braziller, p. 15.

3   Ana Monteiro Ferreira, *The Demise of the Inhuman: Afrocentricity, Modernism, and Postmodernism*. Albany: SUNY Press, 2014; Reiland Rabaka, *Africana Critical Theory: Reconstructing the Black Radical Tradition, from W.E.B. Du Bois and C.L.R. James to Frantz Fanon and Amilcar Cabral*. New York: Lexington, 2010; Christel Temple, *Literary Pan Africanism: History, Context, and Criticism*. Carolina Press, 2004; Michael

Tillotson, *Invisible Jim Crow: Contemporary Ideological Threats to the Internal Security of African Americans,* Trenton: African World Press, 2011.

4　Marcus Garvey, *Message to the People,* edited by Tony Martin. Majority Press, 1990, Lesson 1, p. 1.

5　Kariamu Welsh, "Commonalities in African Dance," in M. K. Asante and K. W. Asante, eds., *African Cutlure: Rhythms of Unity.* Westport: Greenwood, 1985.

6　Maulana Karenga, *Introduction to Black Studies.* Los Angeles: University of Sankore Press, 2010.

7　Cheikh Anta Diop, *Civilization or Barbarism: An Authentic Anthropology.* Chicago: Chicago Review Press, 1991.

8　Alexander Pope, *An Essay on Man.* New York: Oliver and Munroe, 1951.

9　Stephen Jay Gould, The Mismeasure of Man. New York: Norton, p. 31.

10　Georg Hegel, Reason in History. Trans. R. Hortmann. Indianapolis: Bobbs-Merrill, 1982. I have quoted several pieces from Hegel throughout the following discussion. They refer to this copy of his text.

11　Marimba Ani, *Yurugu: An African-Centered Critique of European Cultural Thought and Behavior.* Trenton: Africa World Press, 1994.

12　Cheikh Anta Diop, *The African Origin of Civilization: Myth or Reality.* Chicago: Lawrence Hill, 1974, p. 102.

13　Yoshitaka Miike, "An Asiacentric Reflection on Eurocentric Bias in Communication Theory." *Communication Monographs* 74 (2007), pp. 272-278. This is a brilliant and pointed essay by one of the most intelligent writers in communication. Miike's starting point is how own Asian culture as it should be and from that vantage point he argues that numerous ancient philosophers of Asia emphasized the idea of clarity over the idea of rationality or reason. His work has elicited some negative reactions, even from Asians, but he has maintained an elegant position in intellectual history by speaking of the need to re-assess the imposition of Europe on everything.

14　Karl Popper, "A Reply," in Imre Lakatos and Alan Musgrave, eds., *Criticism and the Growth of Knowledge.* Cambridge: Cambridge University Press, 1970.

15　Paul Feyerabend, *Against Method.* New York: Routledge, 1988.

16　C. T. Keto, *The Africa-Centered Perspective of History.* Blackwood, New Jersey: K. A. Publications, 1989, p. 15.

17   Keto, p. 15.

18   Lucius Outlaw, "Africology: Normative Theory," Symposium on Africology at the Department of African American Studies, University of Wisconsin, Milwaukee, *Proceedings*, April 24, 1987, p. 42. At this symposium organized by Winston Van Horne and attended by Maulana Karenga, Molefi Kete Asante, Patrick Bellegarde-Smith and several other invited scholars, Van Horne proposed the name Africology for his department. This was a powerful advance in the field. I had used the term "Afrology" in the book *Afrocentricity* in 1980 but agreed to follow Van Horne's lead in the use of Africology.

CHAPTER TWO

1   George F. Brooks, "A Provisional Historical Schema for Western Africa Based on Seven Climate Periods: Ca 9000 BC to the 19th Century," *Cahiers d'Etudes Africaines,* 101-102, XXVI, 1-2, 1986, pp. 32-66.

2   See Maulana Karenga and Jacob Carruthers, Kemetic Worldview: Essays in Ancient Egyptian Studies. Los Angeles: University of Sankore Press, 1984.

3   Herodotus, *History of Egypt*. Re-translated and edited by Molefi Kete Asante. Philadelphia: Ramses, 2013.

4   Eugen Strouhal, "Evidence of the Early Penetration of Negroes into Predynastic Egypt," Journal of African History, 12 (1), 1971, pp. 4-7.

5   Strouhal, p. 3.

6   Anthony Browder, "Karakhamun: Nubian Priest of the 25th Dynasty," Cheikh Anta Diop International Conference, Philadelphia, October, 2012.

7   Anthony Browder, "Looking for Karakhamun," International Cheikh Anta Diop Conference, October 2012, Philadelphia.

8   Mary Lefkowitz, *Not Out of Africa: How Afrocentrism Became An Excuse to Teach Myth as History*. New York: Basic Books, 1996. Lefkowitz' work was championed by the intellectual rightwing as a champion of the Eurocentric "strike back" against Afrocentric historians, black or white.

9   Molefi Kete Asante, *The Painful Demise of Eurocentrism*. Trenton: Africa World Press, 2005. This book is a polemic and an analysis and the intent of the work is to demonstrate the inaccurate interpretations given by Mary Lefkowitz in her attack on Africa agency and history. Clearly, *The Painful Demise of Eurocentrism*, uses Lefkowitz' own arguments to show

how she misjudged documents and made errors of interpretation based on a monocultural analysis.

10   G. Brunton and G. Caton-Thompson, *The Badarian Civilization and Predynastic Remains Near Badari*. London: Quaritch, 1928, pp. 40-42.

11   Strouhal, p. 7.

12   *DNA Tribes Digest*, February 1, 2013, p. 4.

13   Spencer Wells, *The Journey of Man: A Genetic Odyssey*. New York: Random House, 2003.

14   Herodotus, *The History of Egypt*.

15   Cheikh Anta Diop, *The African Origin of Civilization*. Chicago: Lawrence Hill, 1974.

16   Jacob Carruthers, *Essays in Ancient Egyptian Studies*. Los Angeles: University of Sankore Press, 1984, p. 29. The language of ancient Egypt is now being called ciKam or mdwKam meaning essentially the "language of Kemet."

17   Carruthers, p. 29.

18   G. Kubik, "African Graphic Systems," *Muntu*, vol 1, no. 4-5, 1986.

19   G. Kubik, "African Graphic Systems: A Reassessment," in *Mitteilungan der Anthropologischen Gesellscraft in Wien*. Vols. 114 and 115, 1984-1985. F. Jaritz, "Uber Bahnen auf Billardrischen-Oder. *Eine Mathematishch-Statatische Sektion*, Research Center A 8010, Graz, Austria, 1983.

20   G. Niangaran-Bouah, *L'Univers Akan des Poids a Peser L'Or*. Abidjan: Les Nouvelles Editions Africaines, 1984. In addition to this discussion, it is important to understand the Adinkra system of symbols. The Akan Sankofa system is based upon the tradition of Adinkra, a famous king of Gyaman, now Ivory Coast. Adinkra angered Asantehene Bonsu-Panyin by trying to copy the Golden Stool. Adinkra was slain in a war with the Asantehene. The term "Sankofa" is often used to refer to the Adinkra symbols but *Sankofa* is only one of the symbols. Adinkra means literally "good-bye" or "farewell."

21   Niangaran-Bouah, p. 6.

22   Ama Mazama, *The Afrocentric Paradigm*. Trenton: Africa World Press, 2003, p. 5.

23   Theophile Obenga, *Pour une Nouvelle Histoire*. Paris: Presence Africain, p. 58.

24   Kubik, p. 25.

25   Cheikh Anta Diop, *The African Origin of Civilization: Myth or Reality?* Paris: Presence Africain, p. 43.

26   Diop, p. 40.

27   Cheikh Anta Diop, *Parente genetique de l'Egyptien Pharaonique et des Langues Negro-Africains.* Dakar: IFAN, 1977.

28   Maulana Karenga, *The Husia.* Los Angeles: University of Sankore, 1984, p. xiv.

29   Henri Frankfort, *Ancient Egyptian Religion.* New York: Harper and Row, 1961, p. 81.

30   Marcel Griaule, *Conversations with Ogotommeli.* New York: Oxford University Press, 1978.

31   Maulana Karenga, *Maat: The Moral Ideal in Ancient Egypt.* New York: Routledge; Willie Cannon-Brown, *Nefer: The Aesthetic Ideal in Ancient Egypt.* New York: Routledge

CHAPTER THREE

1   Albert Churchward, *The Signs and Symbols of Primordial Man.* Westport, Ct.: Greenwood Press, 1978, p. xvi.

2   Martin Bernal, *Black Athena.* New Brunswick: Rutgers University Press, 1987, p. 51.

3   Bernal, p. 52.

4   Bernal, p. 203.

5   Wade Nobles, *Sakhu.* Chicago: Third World Press, 2009.

6   Denis Williams, *Icons and Image.* New York: New York University Press, p. 19.

7   Sigmund Freud, *Civilization and Its Discontents.*

8   Roy Preiswerk and Dominique Perrot, *Ethnocentrism in History.* New York: Nok, 1977, p. 40.

9   Edward Wilmot Blyden, *Christianity, Islam, and the Negro Race.* Edinburgh: Edinburgh University Press, 1967.

10   Al-Amin Mazrui, *The African Condition.* London: Heinemann, 1980.

11   Hailu Habtu, The Fallacy of the "Triple Heritage" Thesis: A Critique. *Issue,* 1984, XIII.

12   Habtu, p. 26-27.

13   Ngugi wa Thiong'o, *Decolonising the Mind*. London: Heinemann, 1986, p. 4.

14   Ngugi, p. 18.

15   Chinweizu, *Decolonizing the African Mind*. London: Sundoor, 1989.

16   Molefi Kete Asante, *Herodotus on Egypt*. Philadelphia: Ramses, 2013.

17   John Jackson, *Introduction to African Civilization*. Secaucus, NJ: Citadel Press, 1974, p. 158.

18   Harry Johnston, *The Ugandan Protectorate*. London: privately published, Volume, p. 473.

19   Quoted by Bernal from Herodotus, *The History*. 2:91-93.

20   Bernal, *Black Athena*, Vol. 1, 1987, p. 203.

21   Edward Said, *Orientalism*. New York: Vintage, 1979, p. 3.

22   Said, p. 6.

23   Said, p. 11.

24   Said, p. 17.

25   Said, p. 53.

26   Sulayman Nyang, *Islam, Christianity, and African Identity*. Brattleboro, Vt.: Amana, 1984, p. 9

27   Nyang, p. 20.

28   Nyang, p. 29.

29   Nyang, p. 48.

30   Nyang, p. 49.

31   Nyang, p. 50

32   Nyang, p. 50

33   MacMichael, 1967, p. 4.

34   MacMichael, p. 12

35   MacMichael, p. 14

36   MacMichael, p. 16

37   MacMichael, p. 21

38   MacMichael, p. 29

39   MacMichael, p. 31

40   Basil Davidson, *The Lost Cities of Africa*. Boston: Little, Brown, and Company, l959, p. 7

41   Albert Churchward, *The Signs and Symbols of Primordial Man*, p. 214.

42   Ibn Khaldun, *The Muqaddimah: An Introduction to History*. Princeton: Princeton University Press, 1967, p. 63.

43   Ibn Khaldun, p. 63.

44   David W. Phillipson, *African Archaeology*. London: Cambridge University Press, 1985, p. 3.

45   Roy Preiswerk and Dominique Perrot, *Ethnocentrism in History*. New York: Nok Publishers, 1977, p. xvi.

46   Preiswerk and Perrot, p. 40.

CHAPTER FOUR

1   Maulana Karenga, *Kawaida Theory*. Los Angeles: Kawaida Press, 1980.

2   Preiswerk and Perrot, p. 46.

3   www.youtube.com/watch?v=6zx9Co3s5Jw

4   Preiswerk and Perrot, p. 46

5   Preiswerk and Perrot, p. 47

6   Preiswerk and Perrot, p. 49

7   Carter G. Woodson, *The Mis-education of the Negro*. Washington: Associated Publishers, 1933, p. 7.

8   Woodson, p. 1.

9   Ralph Ellison, *Invisible Man*. New York: Random House, 1952.

10   Frantz Fanon, *The Wretched of the Earth*. New York: Grove Press, 2005.

11   John Henrik Clarke, "History and the African World," speech given at Miles College, Birmingham, Alabama, April 17, 1983.

12   Frank Tucker, *The White Conscience*. New York: Frederick Ungar Publishing Co., 1968, p. 14. See also Lewis Hanke, *The Spanish Struggle for Justice in the Conquest of the Americas*. Philadelphia, 1949; Lewis Hanke, *Aristotle and the American Indians*. Chicago, 1959.

13   Edward O. Wilson, On *Human Nature*. Cambridge: Harvard University Press, 1978, p. 167.

14   A. Rosenberg, *Sociobiology and the Preemption of Social Science*. Baltimore: John Hopkins University Press, 1980.

15   Arthur Lovejoy, *Great Chain of Being.* New York: Harper and Row, 1960.

16   Diodorus Siculus, *Histoire universelle.* Trans. Abbe Terrason. Book 1:23, 2; Book 1:60, Paris, 1758.; Plato, *Timaeus,* 22, 23; Diogénes Laercc, *Thales,* 43, 24; Jamblicus, *Life of Pythagoras,* 4:18-20; Olympiodorus, *Life of Plato* and Strago, *Description of Egypt,* XVII, I, 29.

17   Josiah A. M. Cobbah "African Values and the Human Rights Debate: An African Perspective" Human Rights Quarterly, Vol. 9, No. 3 (Aug., 1987

18   Clyde Ledbetter, Jr., "A Critical Location of Dissemination Effectiveness in a West African Country: The Case of the African Charter on Human and People's Rights in the Gambia." Doctoral Dissertation, Temple University, 2013.

19   Elisa Nascimento, *Pan Africanism and South America.* Buffglo: Afro-Diaspora, 1979, p. 6., Abdias do Nascimento, *Mixture* or *Massacre: The Genocide of a People.* Buffalo: AfroDiaspora, 1978; and Michael Omi and Howard Winant, *Racial Formation in the United States.* New York: Routledge, 1986.

20   Ronald Walters, "Marxism-Leninism and Black Revolution," *Black Books Bulletin, 5:3,* Fall.

21   Vincent Harding, *There is a River.* New York: Harcourt, Brace, Jovanovich, 1981.

22   Sterling Stuckey, *Slave Culture,* pp. 11-46.

CPSIA information can be obtained at www.ICGtesting.com
Printed in the USA
LVOW10s0743011215

464675LV00001B/28/P